Chambers

Portuguese phrasebook

Bill Martin

Cristina Mendes

Chambers

First published by Chambers Harrap Publishers Ltd 2006
7 Hopetoun Crescent
Edinburgh EH7 4AY

© Chambers Harrap Publishers Ltd 2006

ISBN 0550 10284 1

Editor & Project Manager
Anna Stevenson

Publishing Manager
Patrick White

Prepress
Susan Lawrie
Vienna Leigh

Designed and typeset by Chambers Harrap Publishers Ltd, Edinburgh
Printed and bound by Tien Wah Press (PTE.) LTD., Singapore
Illustrations by Art Explosion

CONTENTS

INTRODUCTION

This brand new English-Portuguese phrasebook from Chambers is ideal for anyone wishing to try out their foreign language skills while travelling abroad. The information is practical and clearly presented, helping you to overcome the language barrier and mix with the locals.

Each section features a list of useful words and a selection of common phrases: some of these you will read or hear, while others will help you to express yourself. The simple phonetic transcription system, specifically designed for English speakers, ensures that you will always make yourself understood.

The book also includes a mini bilingual dictionary of around 4,000 words, so that more adventurous users can build on the basic structures and engage in more complex conversations.

Concise information on local culture and customs is provided, along with practical tips to save you time. After all, you're on holiday – time to relax and enjoy yourself! There is also a food and drink glossary to help you make sense of menus, and ensure that you don't miss out on any of the national or regional specialities.

Remember that any effort you make will be appreciated. So don't be shy – have a go!

ABBREVIATIONS USED IN THIS GUIDE

adj	adjective
adv	adverb
art	article
f	feminine
fpl	feminine plural
m	masculine
mf	masculine and feminine
mpl	masculine plural
n	noun
pron	pronoun
v	verb

PRONUNCIATION

Alphabet

a	*ah* (as in "art")	**j**	*Joh-tUH*	**s**	*ehs*
b	*bay*	**k**	*kah-pUH*	**t**	*tay*
c	*say*	**l**	*ehl*	**u**	*oo* (as in "too")
d	*day*	**m**	*ehm*	**v**	*vay*
e	*eh* (as in "pet")	**n**	*ehn*	**w**	*dooblay-yoo*
f	*ehf*	**o**	*oh* (as in "hot")	**x**	*sheesh*
g	*gay*	**p**	*pay*	**y**	*ee-graygoo* or
h	*UH-gah*	**q**	*kay*		*eh-psee-lon*
i	*ee* (as in "bee")	**r**	*ehRR*	**z**	*zay*

Pronunciation

For every sentence written in Portuguese in this guide, you will find the pronunciation given in italics. If you follow this phonetic transcription, you will be able to make yourself understood in Portuguese. Some Portuguese sounds do not exist in English, and so we have used the following codes to transcribe them:

η   this indicates a nasal sound as in "mine", "ounce", "coin". The nasalization shown by this symbol is always weaker than its preceding vowel, eg **mãe** *maeeη*, **pão** *pouη*, **põe** *poiη*

J   similar to the "s" in "vision", eg **justo** *Joos-too*, **jogar** *Joo-gar*

RR   similar to the "ch" in the Scottish word "loch", although it can also be pronounced as a strongly rolled "r", eg **carro** *kah-RRoo*, **rato** *RRah-too*

UH   similar to the "u" in "cut", eg **maçã** *mUH-sUHη*, **cama** *kUH-mUH*

Note that the bold text indicates that you should stress that syllable.

In general, the Portuguese tend to be quite formal and polite when speaking to others. They address people using the terms **Senhor** or **Senhora/Dona**, and consider it important to use the correct professional titles. When they are introduced to someone they usually shake hands, although women and young people often greet each other with a kiss on each cheek. Younger people tend to be less formal, addressing new acquaintances by their first names and using the familiar form of address (**tu**) with each other.

The basics

bye adeus *UH-dae-oosh*, chau *tchah-oo*
excuse me desculpe *desh-kool-p*, com licença *kom lee-sain-sUH*
good afternoon boa tarde *bo-UH tahr-d*
good evening boa noite *bo-UH noy-t*
good morning bom dia *bom dee-ya*
goodbye adeus *UH-dae-oosh*
goodnight boa noite *bo-UH noy-t*
hello/hi olá *oh-lah*
maybe talvez *tahl-vaysh*
no não *noun*
OK ok *oh-kay*
pardon perdão *per-doun*, desculpe *desh-kool-p*
please por favor *poor fUH-vor*, se faz favor *s-fahsh fUH-vor*
sorry desculpe *desh-kool-p*
thanks/thank you obrigado/obrigada *oh-bree-gah-doo/oh-bree-gah-dUH*
yes sim *seen*

Expressing yourself

I'd like ...
queria ...
*ke-**ree**-ya ...*

we'd like ...
queríamos ...
*ke-**ree**-ya-moosh ...*

do you want ...?
quer ...?
kehr ...?

do you have ...?
tem/têm ...?
*taim/**tae**-aim ...?*

is there a ...?
há um/uma ...?
*ah oom/**oo**-mUH ...?*

are there any ...?
há algum/alguma ...?
*ah ahl-**goom**/ahl-**goo**-mUH ...?*

how ...?/how?
como é que ...?/como?
*ko-moo eh ke ...?/**ko**-moo?*

why ...?/why?
por que é que ...?/porquê?
*poor ke eh ke ...?/poor-**kae**?*

when ...?
quando ...?
kwUHn-doo ...?

what ...?/what?
o que é que ...?/o quê?
*oo ke eh ke ...?/oo **kae**?*

where is ...?
onde é/fica ...?
*on-d eh/**fee**-kUH ...?*

where are ...?
onde são/ficam ...?
*on-d souŋ/**fee**-kUHm ...?*

how much is it?
quanto custa?
*kwUHn-too **koosh**-tUH?*

what is it?
o que é (que é)?
*oo ke **eh** (ke eh)?*

where are the toilets, please?
por favor, (pode dizer-me) onde são as casas de banho?
*poor fUH-**vor**, (**poh**-d dee-**zaer**-mae) on-d souŋ UHsh **kah**-sUHsh dae **bUHn**-yo?*

how are you?
como está?
*ko-moo esh-**tah**?*

fine, thanks
bem, obrigado/obrigada
*baim, oh-bree-**gah**-doo/oh-bree-**gah**-dUH*

do you speak English?
fala inglês?
*fah-lUH een-**glaysh**?*

thanks very much
muito obrigado/obrigada
mooy-too oh-bree-gah-doo/oh-bree-gah-dUH

no, thanks
não, obrigado/obrigada
nouŋ, oh-bree-gah-doo/oh-bree-gah-dUH

yes, please
sim, se faz favor
seeŋ, s-fahsh fUH-vor

you're welcome
de nada, não tem de quê
dae nah-dUH, nouŋ taim dae kae

see you later
até logo
UH-teh loh-goo

see you soon
até já
UH-teh Jah

I'm sorry
peço desculpa
pae-soo desh-kool-pUH

Understanding

aberto	open
atenção	attention
avariado	out of order
cuidado	attention
empurre	push
encerrado	closed
entrada	entrance
entrada livre/grátis	free entry
fechado	closed
fora de serviço	out of order
grátis/gratuito	(for) free
homens (H)	gents
lavabos	toilets
livre	free/vacant
não fumadores	no smoking
não incomodar	do not disturb
ocupado	busy/occupied
perigo	danger
proibido ...	do not ...

puxe	pull
reservado	reserved
saída	exit
senhoras (S)	ladies
WC	toilets

há ...
there's/there are ...

bem-vindo/bem-vinda
welcome

importa-se que ...?
do you mind if ... ?

um momento, por favor
one moment, please

PROBLEMS UNDERSTANDING PORTUGUESE

Expressing yourself

pardon?
perdão?
per-douŋ ?

what?
o quê?
oo kae?

I don't understand
não compreendo
nouŋ kom-prain-doo

could you repeat that, please?
importa-se de repetir?
eem-pohr-tUH-sae dae RRe-pe-teer

could you speak more slowly?
importa-se de falar mais devagar?
eem-pohr-tUH-sae dae fUH-lahr my-sh dae-vUH-gahr?

I understand a little Portuguese
compreendo um pouco o português
kom-prain-doo oom po-koo oo poor-too-gaysh

I can understand Portuguese but I can't speak it
compreendo o português, mas não falo
kom-prain-doo oo poor-too-gaysh, mUHsh nouŋ fah-loo

I hardly speak any Portuguese
o meu português é muito limitado
oo mae-oo poor-too-gaysh eh mooy-too lee-mee-tah-doo

how do you say ... in Portuguese?
como é que se diz ... em português?
koh-moo eh ke se deesh ... aim poor-too-gaysh?

how do you spell it?
como é que se escreve?
ko-moo eh ke se esh-kreh-v?

what's that called in Portuguese?
como é que se chama em português?
ko-moo eh ke se shUH-mUH aim poor-too-gaysh?

could you write it down for me?
importa-se de escrever?
eem-pohr-tUH-sae desh-kre-vehr?

Understanding

percebe português?/entende o português?
do you understand Portuguese?

(deixe que) eu escrevo
I'll write it down for you

significa ...
it means ...

é uma espécie de ...
it's a kind of ...

SPEAKING ABOUT THE LANGUAGE

Expressing yourself

I learned a few words from my phrasebook
aprendi algumas palavras com a ajuda do meu guia de conversação
UH-prain-dee ahl-goo-mUHsh pUH-lah-vrUHsh kom UH UH-Joo-dUH doo mae-oo gee-ya dae kon-ver-sUH-souη

I studied Portuguese for a while but I've forgotten everything
estudei português durante algum tempo mas já esqueci tudo
esh-too-day poor-too-gaysh doo-rUHn-t ahl-goom taim-poo mUHsh Jah esh-keh-see too-doo

I can just about get by
desenrasco-me
dae-zain-RRahsh-koo-mae

I hardly know two words!
não sei quase nada!
nouη say kwah-z nah-dUH!

I find Portuguese a difficult language
português é muito difícil
*poor-too-**gaysh** eh **mooy**-too dee-**fee**-seel*

I know the basics but no more than that
sei algumas coisas básicas, mas pouco mais
*say ahl-**goo**-mUHsh **koy**-zUHsh **bah**-zee-kUHsh, mUHsh **po**-koo **my**-sh*

people speak too quickly for me
as pessoas falam demasiado depressa
*UHsh pe-**soh**-UHsh **fah**-lUHm dae-mUH-zee-**ya**-doo dae-**preh**-sUH*

Understanding

tem uma boa pronúncia
you have a good accent

fala muito bem português
you speak very good Portuguese

ASKING THE WAY

Expressing yourself

excuse me, can you tell me where the ... is, please?
desculpe, pode dizer-me onde é ...?
*desh-**kool**-p, **poh**-d dee-**zaer**-mae **on**-d eh ...?*

which way is it to ...?
qual é o caminho para ...?
*kwahl eh oo kUH-**meen**-yo pUH-**rUH** ...?*

can you tell me how to get to ...?
podia dizer-me como chego a ...?
*poo-**dee**-ya dee-**zehr**-mae **ko**-moo **shae**-goo UH ...?*

is there a ... near here?
há ... aqui perto?
*ah ... UH-**kee** pehr-too?*

could you show me on the map?
podia dizer-me onde fica no mapa?
*poo-**dee**-ya dee-**zehr**-mae **on**-d **fee**-kUH noo **mah**-pUH?*

is it far/near?
é muito longe/perto?
eh mooy-too lon-Je/pehr-too?

I'm looking for …
procuro …
proh-koo-roo …

I'm lost
estou perdido/perdida
esh-to per-dee-doo/per-dee-dUH

Understanding

à direita	right
à esquerda	left
descer	to go down
seguir	to follow
sempre a direito	to keep going
sempre em frente	straight ahead
subir	to go up
virar	to turn
voltar para trás	to turn back

está a pé ou de carro?
are you on foot or in a car?

são cinco minutos de carro/a pé
it's five minutes by car/on foot

é a primeira/segunda rua à esquerda
it's the first/second street on the left

vire à direita na rotunda
turn right at the roundabout

vire à esquerda no semáforo/nos sinais de trânsito
turn left at the traffic lights

siga sempre em frente
go straight ahead

saia na saída seguinte
take the next exit

é pertinho/não fica longe
it's quite close/it's not far

é bastante longe
it's quite far

é mesmo ali/é já ao virar da esquina
it's just round the corner

GETTING TO KNOW PEOPLE

The basics

bad	mau/má *mah-oo/mah*
beautiful	lindo/linda *leen-doo/leen-dUH*
boring	aborrecido/aborrecida *UH-boo-RRe-see-doo/ UH-boo-RRe-see-dUH*
cheap	barato/barata *bUH-rah-too/bUH-rah-tUH*
expensive	caro/cara *kah-roo/kah-rUH*
good	bom/boa *bom/bo-UH*
great	espectacular *esh-peh-tUH-koo-lahr*
interesting	interessante *een-te-re-sUHn-t*
not bad	não está mal *noun esh-tah mah-l*
pretty	bonito/bonita *boo-nee-too/boo-nee-tUH*
ugly	feio/feia *fay-oo/fay-UH*
(very) well	(muito) bem *(mooy-too) baim*
to hate	detestar *de-tesh-tahr*
to like	gostar (de) *goosh-tahr (dae)*
to love	adorar *UH-doo-rahr*

INTRODUCING YOURSELF AND FINDING OUT ABOUT OTHER PEOPLE

Expressing yourself

my name's ...
chamo-me ...
shUH-moo-mae ...

what's your name?
como se chama?
ko-moo se shUH-mUH?

how do you do!
como está?
ko-moo esh-tah?

pleased to meet you!
muito prazer!
mooy-too prUH-zer!

this is my husband
(este é) o meu marido
(aesh-t eh) oo mae-oo mUH-ree-doo

this is my partner, Karen
(esta é) a minha companheira, Karen
*(aesh-tUH eh) UH **meen**-ya kom-pUHn-**yay**-rUH, Karen*

I'm English
sou inglês/inglesa
*so een-**glaysh**/een-**glae**-zUH*

we're Welsh
somos galeses/galesas
*so-moosh gUH-**lae**-zesh/gUH-**lae**-zUHsh*

I'm from …
sou de …
so dae …

where are you from?
de onde é?
*dae **on**-d eh?*

how old are you?
quantos anos tem?
kwUHn-toosh UH-noosh taim?

I'm 22
tenho 22 (anos)
*tain-yo **veen**-t ee **doy**-eesh (UH-noosh)*

what do you do for a living?
o que é que faz?
oo ke eh ke fahsh?

are you a student?
é estudante?
*eh esh-too-**dUHn**-t?*

I work
trabalho
*trUH-**bahl**-yoo*

I'm studying law
estou a estudar Direito
*esh-**to** UH esh-too-**dahr** dee-**ray**-too*

I'm a teacher
sou professor/professora
*so proo-fe-**sor**/proo-fe-**so**-rUH*

I stay at home with the children
trabalho em casa e tomo conta das crianças
*trUH-**bahl**-yoo aim kah-sUH ee **toh**-moo **kon**-tUH dUHsh kree-**UHn**-sUHsh*

I work part-time
trabalho part-time
*trUH-**bahl**-yoo part-time*

I work in marketing
trabalho em marketing
*trUH-**bahl**-yoo aim marketing*

I'm retired
estou reformado/reformada
*esh-**to** RRe-foor-**mah**-doo/RRe-foor-**mah**-dUH*

I'm self-employed
trabalho por conta própria
*trUH-**bahl**-yoo poor **kon**-tUH **proh**-pree-ya*

I have two children
tenho dois filhos
tain-yo doy-eesh feel-yoosh

we don't have any children
não temos filhos
noun̴ tae-moosh feel-yoosh

two boys and a girl
dois rapazes e uma rapariga
doy-eesh RRUH-pah-zesh ee oo-mUH RRUH-pUH-ree-gUH

a boy of five and a girl of two
um menino de cinco anos e uma menina de dois anos
oom mae-nee-noo dae seen-koo UH-noosh ee oo-mUH mae-nee-nUH dee doy-eesh UH-noosh

have you ever been to Britain?
conhece a Grã-Bretanha?
kon-yeh-sae UH grUH bre-tUHn-yUH?

Understanding

é inglês/inglesa?
are you English?

também estamos de férias
we're on holiday too

conheço bem a Inglaterra
I know England quite well

um dia adorava ir à Escócia
I'd love to go to Scotland one day

TALKING ABOUT YOUR STAY

Expressing yourself

I'm here on business
estou aqui a negócios
esh-to UH-kee UH nae-goh-see-oosh

we're on holiday
estamos de férias
esh-tUH-moosh dae feh-ree-UHsh

I arrived three days ago
cheguei há três dias
shae-gay ah traysh dee-UHsh

we've been here for a week
estamos cá há uma semana
esh-tUH-moosh kah ah oo-mUH s-mUH-nUH

I'm only here for a long weekend
estou aqui apenas um fim-de-semana prolongado
*esh-**to** UH-kee UH-**pae**-nUHsh oom feem dae s-**mUH**-nUH pro-lon-**gah**-doo*

we're just passing through
estamos só de passagem
*esh-**tUH**-moosh soh dae pUH-**sah**-Jaim*

this is our first time in Portugal
é a primeira vez que visitamos Portugal
*eh UH pree-**may**-rUH vaysh ke vee-zee-**tUH**-moosh poor-too-**gahl***

we're here to celebrate our wedding anniversary
viemos para festejar o aniversário do nosso casamento
*vee-**eh**-moosh pUH-rUH fesh-tae-**Jahr** oo UH-nee-ver-**sah**-ryoo doo **noh**-soo kUH-sUH-**main**-too*

we're on our honeymoon
estamos em lua-de-mel
*esh-**tUH**-moosh aim **loo**-UH dae mehl*

we're here with friends
estamos com uns amigos
*esh-**tUH**-moosh kom oonsh UH-**mee**-goosh*

we're touring around the Algarve
estamos a visitar o Algarve
*esh-**tUH**-moosh UH vee-zee-**tahr** oo ahl-**gahr**-v*

we managed to get a cheap flight
conseguimos um voo barato
*kon-sae-**gee**-moosh oom **vo**-oo bUH-**rah**-too*

we're thinking about buying a house here
estamos a pensar comprar uma casa aqui
*esh-**tUH**-moosh UH pain-**sahr** kom-**prahr** oo-mUH **kah**-sUH UH-**kee***

Understanding

boa estadia!	enjoy your stay!
bom resto de férias!	enjoy the rest of your holiday!

é a primeira vez que visita Portugal?
is this your first time in Portugal?

16

quanto tempo vai ficar?
how long are you staying?

está a gostar?
do you like it here?

já foi a …?
have you been to …?

STAYING IN TOUCH

Expressing yourself

we should stay in touch
porque não nos mantemos em contacto?
poor-ke noun noosh mUHn-tae-moosh aim kon-tah-too?

here's my address, if ever you come to Britain
este é o meu endereço, se um dia resolver visitar a Grã-Bretanha
aesh-t eh oo mae-oo ain-dae-rae-soo, sae oom dee-ya RRe-zohl-vaer vee-zee-tahr UH grUH bre-tUHn-yUH

Understanding

dá-me o seu endereço/a sua direcção?
will you give me your address?

tem endereço de e-mail?
do you have an e-mail address?

se nos quiser visitar é muito bem vindo/vinda
you're always welcome to come and stay with us here

EXPRESSING YOUR OPINION

Some informal expressions

é um espanto it's amazing
foi divertidíssimo it was loads of fun
foi muito giro it was great fun
foi um pouco seca it was a bit boring

Expressing yourself

I really like ...
gosto muito de ...
gohsh-too mooy-too dae ...

I really liked ...
gostei imenso de ...
goosh-tay ee-main-soo dae ...

I don't like ...
não gosto de ...
nouη gohsh-too dae ...

I didn't like ...
não gostei de ...
nouη goosh-tay dae ...

I love ...
adoro ...
UH-doh-roo ...

I loved ...
adorei ...
UH-doo-ray ...

I would like ...
gostaria de ...
goosh-tUH-ree-ya dae ...

I would have liked ...
teria gostado de ...
te-ree-ya goosh-tah-doo dae ...

I find it ...
acho ...
ah-shoo ...

I found it ...
achei ...
UH-shay ...

it's lovely
é uma maravilha
eh oo-mUH mUH-rUH-veel-yUH

it was lovely
foi uma maravilha
foy-ee oo-mUH mUH-rUH-veel-yUH

I agree
concordo
kon-kohr-doo

I don't agree
não concordo
nouη kon-kohr-doo

I don't know
não sei
nouη say

I don't mind
não me importo
nouη mae eem-pohr-too

I don't like the sound of it
não me agrada
nouη mae UH-grah-dUH

it sounds interesting
parece interessante
pUH-reh-sae een-te-re-sUHn-t

it really annoys me
irrita-me profundamente
ee-RRee-tUH-mae pro-foon-dUH-main-t

it was boring
foi aborrecido/aborrecida
foy-ee UH-boo-RRe-see-doo/UH-boo-RRe-see-dUH

it's a rip-off
é uma roubalheira
eh oo-mUH ro-bUHl-yay-rUH

it gets very busy at night
à noite há muita animação
ah noy-t ah mooy-tUH UH-nee-mUH-souη

it's very busy
tem muita gente
taim mooy-tUH Jain-t

it's very quiet
é muito tranquilo
eh mooy-too trUHn-kwee-loo

I really enjoyed myself
diverti-me imenso
dee-vaer-tee-mae ee-main-soo

we had a great time
divertimo-nos imenso
dee-vaer-tee-moo-noosh ee-main-soo

there was a really good atmosphere
o ambiente era excelente
oo UHm-bee-ain-t eh-rUH esh-sae-lain-t

we met some nice people
conhecemos pessoas muito simpáticas
kon-yae-sae-moosh pe-so-UHsh mooy-too seem-pah-tee-kUHsh

we found a great hotel
encontrámos um hotel excelente
ain-kon-trah-moosh oom oh-tehl esh-sae-lain-t

Understanding

gosta de ...?
do you like ...?

divertiram-se?
did you enjoy yourselves?

devia ir a ...
you should go to ...

recomendo ...
I recommend ...

é uma zona muito bonita
it's a lovely area

não há muitos turistas
there aren't too many tourists

não vão ao fim-de-semana, há demasiada gente
don't go at the weekend, it's too busy

não é tão bom como dizem
it's a bit overrated

TALKING ABOUT THE WEATHER

Some informal expressions

chove a potes it's pouring down
está um frio de rachar it's freezing
está um gelo it's freezing cold
hoje está um calor de morrer today is a real scorcher

Expressing yourself

what is the weather forecast for tomorrow?
qual é a previsão do tempo para amanhã?
kwahl eh UH pre-vee-soun doo taim-poo pUH-rUH ah-mUHn-yUH?

it's going to be nice
vai estar bom
vaee esh-tahr bom

it isn't going to be nice
não vai estar muito bom
noun vaee esh-tahr mooy-too bom

it's really hot
está muito calor
esh-tah mooy-too kUH-lor

it gets cold at night
à noite arrefece bastante
ah noy-t UH-RRe-feh-se bUHsh-tUHn-t

the weather was beautiful
o tempo esteve uma maravilha
oo taim-poo esh-tae-v oo-mUH mUH-rUH-veel-yUH

it rained a few times
choveu algumas vezes
shoo-vae-oo ahl-goo-mUHsh vae-zesh

there was a thunderstorm
houve trovoada
o-v troo-voo-ah-dUH

it's been lovely all week
o tempo esteve muito bom toda a semana
oo taim-poo esh-tae-v mooy-too bom to-dUH UH s-mUH-nUH

it's very humid here
o tempo aqui é muito húmido
oo taim-poo UH-kee eh mooy-too oo-mee-doo

we've been lucky with the weather
tivemos sorte com o tempo
tee-vae-moosh sohr-t kom oo taim-poo

Understanding

parece que vai chover
it looks as if it's going to rain

prevêem bom tempo para o resto da semana
they've forecast good weather for the rest of the week

amanhã vai estar calor outra vez
it will be hot again tomorrow

TRAVELLING

The basics

airport	aeroporto *UH-eh-roh-por-too*
boarding	embarque *aim-bahr-k*
boarding card	cartão de embarque *kUHr-touŋ daim-bahr-k*
boat	barco *bahr-koo*
bus	autocarro *ow-toh-kah-RRoo*, carreira *kUH-RRay-rUH*
bus station	(estação) rodoviária *(esh-tUH-souŋ) RRoh-doh-vee-ah-ryUH*
bus stop	paragem de autocarro *pUH-rah-Jaim dow-toh-kah-RRoo*
car	carro *kah-RRoo*, automóvel *ow-too-moh-vel*
coach	(bus) autocarro *ow-toh-kah-RRoo*; (on train) camionete *kah-myo-neh-t*
ferry	barco *bahr-koo*, ferry *feh-RRee*
flight	voo *vo-oo*
gate	porta (de embarque) *pohr-tUH (daim-bahr-k)*
left-luggage (office)	depósito de bagagem *dae-poh-zee-too dae bUH-gah-Jaim*
luggage	bagagem *bUH-gah-Jaim*
map	mapa *mah-pUH*
motorway	auto-estrada *ow-toh-sh-trah-dUH*
passport	passaporte *pah-sUH-pohr-t*
plane	avião *UH-vee-ouŋ*
platform	linha *leen-ya*
railway station	estação de caminhos-de-ferro *esh-tUH-souŋ dae kUH-meen-yosh dae feh-RRoo*, estação de comboios *esh-tUH-souŋ dae kom-boh-yoosh*
return (ticket)	bilhete de ida e volta *beel-yae-t dee-dUH ee vohl-tUH*
road	estrada *esh-trah-dUH*
shuttle bus	autocarro de ligação *ow-toh-kah-RRoo dae lee-gUH-souŋ*, navete *nah-veh-t*
single (ticket)	bilhete só de ida *beel-yae-t soh dee-dUH*
street	rua *RRoo-UH*
streetmap	mapa das ruas *mah-pUH dUHsh RRoo-UHsh*

TRAVELLING

taxi	táxi *tahk-see*
terminal	terminal *ter-mee-nahl*
ticket	bilhete *beel-yae-t*
timetable	horário *oh-rah-ryoo*
town centre	centro da cidade *sain-troo dUH see-dah-d*
train	comboio *kom-boh-yoo*
tram	eléctrico *ee-leh-tree-koo*
tram stop	paragem do eléctrico *pUH-rah-Jaim doo ee-leh-tree-koo*
underground	metro *meh-troo*, metropolitano *mae-troo-poo-lee-tUH-noo*
underground station	estação do metro *esh-tUH-souŋ doo meh-troo*
to book	reservar *RRae-zer-vahr*
to check in	fazer o check-in *fUH-zaehr oo sheh-keen*
to hire	alugar *UH-loo-gahr*

Expressing yourself

where can I buy tickets for ...?
onde posso comprar bilhetes para ...?
on-d poh-soo kom-prahr beel-yae-tsh pUH-rUH ...?

a ticket to ..., please
um bilhete para ..., se faz favor
oom beel-yae-t pUH-rUH ..., s-fahsh fUH-vor

I'd like to book a ticket
quero reservar um bilhete
keh-roo RRae-zer-vahr oom beel-yae-t

how much is a ticket to ...?
quanto custa um bilhete para ...?
kwUHn-too koosh-tUH oom beel-yae-t pUH-rUH ...?

are there any concessions for students?
há descontos para estudantes?
ah desh-kon-toosh pUH-rUH esh-too-dUHn-tesh?

could I have a timetable, please?
podia dar-me um horário, se faz favor?
poo-dee-ya dahr-mae oom oh-rah-ryoo, s-fahsh fUH-vor?

is there an earlier/later one?
há algum(a) mais cedo/mais tarde?
*ah ahl-**goom**(-UH) my-sh sae-doo/my-sh **tahr**-d?*

how long does the journey take?
quanto tempo demora (a viagem)?
*kwUHn-too **taim**-poo dae-**moh**-rUH (UH vee-ah-Jaim)?*

is this seat free?
(este lugar) está vago/livre?
*(**aesh**-t loo-**gahr**) esh-**tah** vah-goo/**lee**-vre?*

I think this is my seat
creio que este é o meu lugar
*kray-oo ke **aesh**-t eh oo **mae**-oo loo-**gahr***

sorry, there's someone sitting here
desculpe, está ocupado
*desh-**kool**-p, esh-**tah** oh-koo-**pah**-doo*

could I open/close the window?
posso abrir/fechar a janela?
*poh-soo UH-**breer**/fe-**shahr** UH JUH-**neh**-lUH?*

Understanding

Making sense of abbreviations

3i	terceira idade	senior citizen
AP	comboio rápido Alfa Pendular	fast rail service (reserved seats only)
BUC	bilhete único de coroa	metro ticket
C	criança	child
CP	Caminhos-de-Ferro Portugueses	Portuguese railways
IC	comboio rápido intercidades	intercity train
IR	comboio inter-regional	inter-region train
R	comboio regional	regional train
RNE	Rede (Nacional) de Expressos	intercity bus service
RP	reformados e pensionistas	retired and pensioners

atrasado	delayed
bilhetes	tickets
cancelado	cancelled
chegadas	arrivals
entrada	entrance
entrada proibida	no entry
fumadores	smoking
informações	information
não fumadores	non-smoking
partidas	departures
saída	exit
WC	toilets
WC Homens	gents
WC Senhoras	ladies

BY PLANE

The Portuguese airline **TAP** operates several flights a day from the UK to Lisbon, Porto and Faro (in the Algarve), as well as to Funchal (Madeira). **SATA** flies to the Azores, Funchal and mainland Portugal, while **Portugália** provides mainly domestic flights. The number of flights available, and the cost, vary according to the time of year (prices are higher at Christmas and during the summer). As well as the major UK carriers, several budget airlines now fly to Portugal.

Expressing yourself

where's the British Airways check-in?
onde fica o check-in da British Airways?
on-d fee-kUH oo sheh-keen dUH British Airways?

I've got an e-ticket
tenho um bilhete electrónico
tain-yoo oom beel-yae-t ee-leh-troh-nee-koo

one suitcase and one piece of hand luggage
uma mala e um saco de mão
oo-mUH mah-lUH ee oom sah-koo dae mouŋ

what time do we board?
a que horas é o embarque?
UH ke oh-rUHsh eh oo aim-bahr-k?

I'd like to confirm my return flight
quero confirmar o meu voo de regresso
keh-roo con-feer-mahr oo mae-oo vo-oo dae RRae-greh-soo

one of my suitcases is missing
falta-me uma mala
fahl-tUH-mae oo-mUH mah-lUH

my luggage hasn't arrived
a minha bagagem não chegou
UH meen-ya bUH-gah-Jaim nouŋ shae-go

the plane was two hours late
o avião chegou com duas horas de atraso
oo UH-vee-ouŋ shae-go com doo-UHsh oh-rUHsh dUH-trah-zoo

I've missed my connection
perdi a ligação
per-dee UH lee-gUH-souŋ

I've left something on the plane
deixei uma coisa no avião
day-shaee oo-mUH koy-zUH noo UH-vee-ouŋ

I want to report the loss of my luggage
gostaria de participar a perda da minha bagagem
goosh-tUH-ree-ya dae pUHr-tee-see-pahr UH paer-dUH dUH meen-ya bUH-gah-Jaim

Understanding

alfândega	customs
balcão de registo de bagagem	luggage check-in counter
classe económica	economy class
classe executiva	business class

controlo de passaportes — passport control
controlo de segurança — security check
embarque imediato — immediate boarding
mercadorias a declarar — goods to declare
 (canal vermelho)
nada a declarar (canal verde) — nothing to declare
passageiro frequente — frequent flyer
recolha de bagagem — luggage reclaim
sala de embarque — departure lounge
voos domésticos — domestic flights

queira aguardar na sala de embarque
please wait in the departure lounge

deseja um lugar ao lado da janela ou do corredor?
would you like a window seat or an aisle seat?

quanta bagagem tem?
how many bags do you have?

foi o próprio/a própria a fazer as suas malas?
did you pack all your bags yourself?

alguém lhe pediu para transportar alguma coisa?
has anyone given you anything to take onboard?

(a sua bagagem) tem um excesso de cinco quilos
your luggage is five kilos over

aqui tem o seu cartão de embarque
here's your boarding card

o embarque é à(s) …
boarding will begin at …

queira dirigir-se à porta de embarque número …
please proceed to gate number …

é a última chamada para …
this is the final call for …

**pode ligar para este número para saber se a sua bagagem
 chegou**
you can call this number to check that your luggage has arrived

BY TRAIN, COACH, BUS, UNDERGROUND, TRAM

Rail travel in Portugal is relatively cheap compared to elsewhere in Europe. Children under the age of 4 travel free, while 4- to 11-year-olds can get half-price tickets. Concessions are available for groups (of ten people and over), students and retired people. Second-class travel is 40 per cent cheaper than first-class. If you're planning to do a lot of travelling around the country, you can buy a tourist ticket which entitles you to unlimited travel over a 7-, 14-, or 21-day period (subject to advance booking). For journeys within Portugal, you can buy a **Euro domino** pass which allows you to travel for three, four, five, six, seven or eight days within a calendar month, and there are discounts for those under 26. Tickets and passes can be bought at the station. Fast trains (the Lisbon–Porto route) are known as **Alfas** and **Intercidades** link the major cities.

The Lisbon metro (underground) has four lines covering the city centre and the suburbs. It runs from 6.30am to 1am. Multitrip tickets, day passes and return or two-trip tickets can all be bought from the station ticket offices or machines. Tourist passes are also available and can be used for four or seven days on all forms of public transport.

Buses are a little more expensive than the metro. Tickets can be bought (for a slightly higher price) from the driver. You can also buy passes for one or three days as well as two-trip or multitrip tickets.

Oporto also has a comprehensive bus and tram system and has recently opened two metro lines. All major cities have good bus networks and in Coimbra there are also trolley buses.

Expressing yourself

can I have a map of the underground, please?
podia dar-me um mapa do metro, se faz favor?
*poo-**dee**-ya **dahr**-mae oom **mah**-pUH doo **meh**-troo, s-**fahsh** fUH-**vor**?*

TRAVELLING

what time is the next train to ...?
a que horas é o próximo comboio para ...?
UH ke oh-rUHsh eh oo proh-see-moo kom-boh-yoo pUH-rUH ...?

what time is the last train?
a que horas é o último comboio?
UH ke oh-rUHsh eh oo ool-tee-moo kom-boh-yoo?

which platform is it for ...?
de que linha parte o comboio para ...?
dae ke leen-ya pahr-t oo kom-boh-yoo pUH-rUH ...?

where can I catch a bus to ...?
onde posso apanhar um autocarro para ...?
on-d poh-soo UH-pUHn-yahr oom ow-toh-kah-RRoo pUH-rUH ...?

which line do I take to get to ...?
qual é a linha para ...?
kwal eh UH leen-ya pUH-rUH ...?

is this the stop for ...?
é esta a paragem para ...?
eh ehsh-tUH UH pUH-rah-Jaim pUH-rUH ...?

is this where the coach leaves for ...?
é daqui que sai o autocarro para ...?
eh dUH-kee ke sah-ee oo ow-toh-kah-RRoo pUH-rUH ...?

can you tell me when I need to get off?
pode dizer-me onde devo sair?
poh-d dee-zer-mae on-d dae-voo sUH-eer?

I've missed my train/bus
perdi o comboio/autocarro que devia apanhar
per-dee oo kom-boh-yoo/ow-toh-kah-RRoo ke dae-vee-ya UH-pUHn-yahr

where are the lockers?
onde são os cacifos?
on-d souŋ oosh kUH-see-foosh?

where is the left-luggage office?
onde é o depósito de bagagem?
on-d eh oo dae-poh-zee-too dae bUH-gah-Jaim?

Understanding

acesso às linhas	to the trains
aerobus	airport shuttle
assinaturas/passes	season tickets
bilhete de 1 dia/5 dias	1/5 day pass
bilhete simples 1 zona/2 zonas	1 zone/2 zones single
bilhete simples 10 unidades	10-trip ticket
bilhete simples/1 viagem	single (ticket)
bilheteira	ticket office
bilhetes para o próprio dia	tickets for travel today
carregamento do cartão de passe	automatic pass or season ticket renewal
dias úteis/sábados/ domingos e feriados	weekdays/Saturdays/Sundays and holidays
longo percurso	long distance
meio bilhete	half
mudança de comboio	change
pré-comprado	pre-paid
primeira classe	first class
(rede) madrugada	night bus
reserva obrigatória de lugar	reserved seats only
reservas	bookings
segunda classe	second class
tarifa de bordo	onboard ticket

há uma paragem um pouco mais à frente à direita
there's a stop a bit further along on the right

tem de mudar em ...
you'll have to change at ...

precisa de apanhar o autocarro número ...
you need to get the number ... bus

este comboio pára nas estações de ...
this train calls at ...

são mais duas paragens
two stops from here

portadores de bilhetes válidos para …
only holders of valid tickets for …(can travel on this train)

não se efectua aos sábados e domingos
no service Saturdays and Sundays

só se efectua às 6.ᵃˢ
Fridays only

BY CAR

When driving in Portugal you must have with you your passport, driving licence (international driving licence or one from your home country), car registration papers or car hire documentation and proof of insurance. Finding a parking space can be difficult in big cities, although many underground car parks are now being built. All motorways have tolls, as do the **25 de Abril** and **Vasco da Gama** bridges in Lisbon. As you approach a toll, a "green lane" is reserved for drivers using the automated electronic payment system.

Drive carefully: some of the main roads are not in very good condition. Petrol is quite expensive. Wearing a seatbelt is compulsory in both the front and the back, and using a mobile phone while driving is illegal. Speed limits are 50 km/h in built-up areas, 90 km/h on main roads and 120 km/h on the motorway.

Taxis are a relatively cheap way to get around. Older cars are black with a green roof, while the more modern ones are beige. If you're travelling out of town, the price of your journey will be calculated per kilometre, and it's advisable to agree on the price in advance. There is an extra charge for luggage and fares are increased at the weekend and on national holidays.

Expressing yourself

where can I park?
onde posso estacionar?
*on-d **poh**-soo esh-tUH-see-oo-**nahr**?*

where can I find a service station?
onde posso encontrar uma estação de serviço?
*on-d **poh**-soo ain-kon-**trahr** oo-**mUH** esh-tUH-**sou**ŋ dae ser-**vee**-soo?*

lead-free petrol, please
gasolina sem chumbo, se faz favor
*gUH-zoo-**lee**-nUH saim **shoom**-boo, s-**fahsh** fUH-vor*

how much is it per litre?
quanto custa por litro?
*kwUHn-too **koosh**-tUH poor **lee**-troo?*

fill up the tank, please
encha o depósito, se faz favor
*ain-shUH oo dae-**poh**-zee-too, s-**fahsh** fUH-vor*

we got stuck in a traffic jam
ficámos presos num engarrafamento
*fee-**kah**-moosh **prae**-zoosh noom ain-gUH-**RRUH**-fUH-**main**-too*

is there a garage near here?
há alguma oficina aqui perto?
*ah ahl-**goo**-mUH oh-fee-**see**-nUH UH-**kee** pehr-too?*

can you help us to push the car?
podem ajudar-nos a empurrar o carro?
*poh-daim UH-Joo-**dahr**-noosh UH aim-poo-**RRahr** oo kah-**RRoo**?*

the engine won't start
o motor não pega
*oo moo-**tor** nouŋ peh-gUH*

the battery's dead
a bateria está descarregada
*UH bUH-te-**ree**-ya esh-**tah** desh-kUH-**RRae**-**gah**-dUH*

I've broken down
tive uma avaria
*tee-v **oo**-mUH UH-vUH-**ree**-ya*

we've run out of petrol
ficámos sem gasolina
*fee-**kah**-moosh saim gUH-zoo-**lee**-nUH*

I've got a puncture and my spare tyre is flat
tenho um furo e o pneu sobresselente está vazio
tain-yo oom foo-roo ee oo pee-nae-oo so-bre-sae-lain-t esh-tah vUH-zee-yo

I've had an accident
tive um acidente
tee-vae oom UH-see-dain-t

I've lost my car keys
perdi as chaves do carro
per-dee UHsh shah-vesh doo kah-RRoo

how long will it take to repair?
quanto tempo é que vai levar a reparar?
kwUHn-too taim-poo eh ke vah-ee lae-vahr UH RRae-pUH-rahr?

◆ Hiring a car

I'd like to hire a car for a week
queria alugar um carro por uma semana
ke-ree-ya UH-loo-gahr oom kah-RRoo poor oo-mUH s-mUH-nUH

an automatic (car)
um carro automático
oom kah-RRoo ow-too-mah-tee-koo

I'd like to take out comprehensive insurance
queria um seguro contra todos os riscos
ke-ree-ya oom sae-goo-roo con-trUH to-doosh oosh RReesh-koosh

◆ Getting a taxi

where can I get a taxi?
onde posso apanhar um táxi?
on-d poh-soo UH-pUHn-yahr oom tahk-see?

I'd like to go to …
para …, se faz favor
pUH-rUH …, s-fahsh fUH-vor

I'd like to book a taxi for 8pm
queria reservar um táxi para as 20 horas
ke-ree-ya RRae-zer-vahr oom tahk-see pUH-rUH UHsh veen-t oh-rUHsh

you can drop me off here, thanks
pode deixar-me aqui, obrigado/obrigada
poh-d day-shahr-mae UH-kee, oh-bree-gah-doo/oh-bree-gah-dUH

how much will it be to go to the airport?
quanto custa daqui para o aeroporto?
kwUHn-too koosh-tUH dUH-kee pUH-rUH oo UH-eh-roh-por-too?

◆ Hitchhiking

I'm going to …
vou para …
vo pUH-rUH …

can you drop me off here?
pode deixar-me aqui?
poh-d day-shar-mae UH-kee?

could you take me as far as …?
pode levar-me até …?
poh-d lae-vahr-mae UH-teh …?

we hitched a lift
apanhámos boleia
UH-pUHn-yah-moosh boo-lay-UH

thanks for the lift
obrigado/obrigada pela boleia
oh-bree-gah-doo/ oh-bree-gah-dUH pae-lUH boo-lay-UH

Understanding

aluguer de automóveis	car hire
área de serviço	service area
circule pela direita	drive in slow lane
completo	full *(car park)*
conserve o talão	keep your ticket
desvio	diversion
espaços livres	spaces *(car park)*
estacionamento proibido	no parking
fim de desvio	end of diversion
fim de obras	end of roadworks
ligue os faróis	turn on your headlights
obras a… km	roadworks… km ahead
outras direcções	other directions
pagar e afixar	pay and display
parque de estacionamento	car park
proibido estacionar	no parking
redução a duas vias	lane closure
reduzir a velocidade	reduce speed

seja prudente	drive carefully
todas as direcções	all directions
trânsito sujeito a demora	traffic subject to delay

BY BOAT

In Lisbon, there are several docks for the barges and ferries that serve the industrial towns on the opposite bank of the Tagus. Tickets are available from the offices in these stations, and there are crossings every 15 minutes or so during the day. River cruises along the Tagus are also available and generally last about two hours. Further north, you can explore the Douro with a variety of themed cruises, for example to see the vineyards at grape-harvesting time, or the blossom of the almond groves in springtime.

Expressing yourself

how long is the crossing?
quanto tempo demora a travessia?
kwUHn-too taim-poo dae-moh-rUH UH trUH-vae-see-ya?

I'm seasick
sinto-me enjoado/enjoada
seen-to-mae ain-Joo-ah-doo/ain-joo-ah-dUH

Understanding

passageiros com título de transporte válido para ...	passengers with a valid ticket for ...
passageiros sem viatura	foot passengers only
pontão	pontoon
primeira/última partida de ...	first/last crossing from ...
próxima partida à(s) ...	next crossing at ...
temporal	bad weather

ACCOMMODATION

The price of accommodation in Portugal drops sharply out of season. In busy areas, it is strongly advisable to book well in advance. You will find plenty of information on hotels in tourist offices; however they don't offer a reservations service, so try contacting one of the **Pousadas** (run by the **Enatur** agency) directly (**www.pousadas.pt**). For rural accommodation, it's essential to book in advance, either through a travel agent or the **ANTER** agency (tel./fax 266 74 45 55). A deposit may be required.

Hotels are ranked by a star system (which can sometimes be misleading). They range from a basic bed and breakfast to the slightly more upmarket **residencial** (more comfortable but often with no restaurant) and right up to the more luxurious **estalagem**. **Pousadas** are luxury hotels run by the State and situated in sites of historic interest, parks or nature reserves.

Rural accommodation is also very varied. **Turismo da habitação** is very popular in the North (particularly in the Minho region), and guests stay on farms or in impressive **solares** (manor houses). If you opt for **turismo rural** you can stay in a rustic cottage, while with **agro-turismo** guests rent a room on a family-run farm, where they can help out if they choose.

Camping on non-authorized sites is illegal in Portugal. If you want to stay on one of the many nationally-run campsites (of which there are over a hundred), you'll have to pay a tax and show your International Camping Carnet.

The basics

bath	banheira *bUHn-yay-rUH*
bathroom	casa-de-banho *kah-sUH dae bUHn-yo*
bathroom with shower	casa-de-banho com chuveiro *kah-sUH dae bUHn-yo kom shoo-vay-roo*
bed	cama *kUH-mUH*
bed and breakfast	*(place)* pensão *pain-souŋ*; *(service)* cama e pequeno-almoço *kUH-mUH ee pe-kae-noo ahl-mo-soo*

cable/satellite television	televisão por cabo/por satélite *te-le-vee-souŋ poor kah-boo/poor sUH-teh-lee-t*
campsite	parque de campismo *pahr-k dae kam-peesh-moo*
caravan	caravana *kUH-rUH-vUH-nUH*
cottage	casa *kah-sUH*, vivenda *vee-vain-dah*
double bed	cama de casal *kUH-mUH dae kUH-sahl*
double room	quarto duplo *kwahr-too doo-ploo*
en-suite bathroom	casa-de-banho privativa *kah-sUH dae bUHn-yo pree-vUH-tee-vUH*
family room	quarto para família *kwahr-too pUH-rUH fUH-mee-lee-ya*, quarto familiar *kwahr-too fUH-mee-lee-ahr*
flat	apartamento *UH-pUHr-tUH-main-too*
full-board	pensão completa *pain-souŋ kom-pleh-tUH*
fully inclusive	com tudo incluído *kom too-doo een-kloo-ee-doo*
guesthouse	pensão *pain-souŋ*, (pensão-)residencial *(pain-souŋ-)RRae-zee-dain-see-ahl*
half-board	meia-pensão *may-UH pain-souŋ*
hotel	hotel *oh-tehl*
key	chave *shah-v*
rent	aluguer *UH-loo-gehr*
self-catering	com cozinha *kom koo-zeen-ya*
shower	chuveiro *shoo-vay-roo*
single bed	cama individual *kUH-mUH een-dee-vee-doo-ahl*, cama de solteiro *kUH-mUH dae sohl-tay-roo*
single room	quarto individual *kwahr-too een-dee-vee-doo-ahl*
tent	tenda *tain-dUH*
toilets	casas-de-banho *kah-sUHsh dae bUHn-yo*, WC *dooblay-yoo say*
twin room	quarto duplo com duas camas *kwahr-too doo-ploo kom doo-UHsh kUH-mUHsh*
youth hostel	pousada da juventude *po-zah-dUH dUH Joo-vain-too-d*
to book	reservar *RRae-zer-vahr*
to rent	alugar *UH-loo-gahr*
to reserve	reservar *RRae-zer-vahr*

37

Expressing yourself

I have a reservation
fiz uma reserva
feesh oo-mUH RRae-zehr-vUH

the name's ...
o nome é ...
oo no-m eh ...

do you take credit cards?
aceita cartão de crédito?
UH-say-tUH kUHr-toun dae kreh-dee-too?

Understanding

aluga-se quarto	room for rent
completo/cheio	full
privado	private
quartos livres	vacancies
recepção	reception
WC	toilets

posso ver o seu passaporte?
could I see your passport, please?

assine aqui, por favor
sign here, please

importa-se de preencher esta ficha?
could you fill in this form?

HOTELS

Expressing yourself

do you have any vacancies?
tem quartos disponíveis?
taim kwahr-toosh deesh-poo-nee-vaysh?

how much is a double room per night?
quanto custa um quarto duplo por noite?
kwUHn-too koosh-tUH oom kwahr-too doo-ploo poor noy-t?

I'd like to reserve a double room/a single room
queria reservar um quarto duplo/individual
ke-ree-ya RRae-zer-vahr oom kwahr-too doo-ploo/een-dee-vee-doo-ahl

for three nights
por três noites
poor traysh noy-tesh

would it be possible to stay an extra night?
é possível ficar mais uma noite?
eh poo-see-vehl fee-kahr my-sh oo-mUH noy-t?

do you have any rooms available for tonight?
tem quartos disponíveis para hoje?
taim kwahr-toosh deesh-poo-nee-vaysh pUH-rUH o-Je?

do you have any family rooms?
tem quartos para família?
taim kwahr-toosh pUH-rUH fUH-mee-lee-ya?

would it be possible to add an extra bed?
seria possível instalar uma cama extra?
sae-ree-ya poo-see-vehl eensh-tUH-lahr oo-mUH kUH-mUH aysh-trUH?

could I see the room first?
posso ver primeiro o quarto?
poh-soo vaer pree-may-roo oo kwahr-too?

do you have anything bigger/quieter?
tem algum maior/mais silencioso?
taim ahl-goom mUH-ee-ohr/my-sh see-lain-see-o-zoo?

could you recommend any other hotels?
pode indicar-me outro hotel?
poh-d een-dee-kahr-mae o-troo oh-tehl?

that's fine, I'll take it
está bem, fico com ele
esh-tah baim, fee-koo kom ae-l

is breakfast included?
inclui o pequeno-almoço?
een-klooy oo pe-kae-noo ahl-mo-soo?

what time do you serve breakfast?
a que horas é o pequeno-almoço?
UH ke oh-rUHsh eh oo pe-kae-noo ahl-mo-soo?

where is the lift?
onde é o elevador?
on-d eh oo ee-le-vUH-dor?

is the hotel near the centre of town?
o hotel fica perto do centro?
*oo oh-**tehl** fee-kUH **pehr**-too doo **sain**-troo?*

what time will the room be ready?
a que horas é que o quarto está pronto?
*UH ke **oh**-rUHsh eh ke oo **kwahr**-too esh-**tah pron**-too?*

the key for room ..., please
a chave do quarto ..., se faz favor
*UH **shah**-v doo **kwahr**-too ..., s-**fahsh** fUH-**vor***

could I have an extra blanket?
é possível obter um cobertor extra?
*eh poo-**see**-vehl ohb-**taer** oom koo-ber-**tor** aysh-trUH?*

the air conditioning isn't working
o ar-condicionado não funciona
*oo ahr kon-dee-see-oo-**nah**-doo noun foon-see-o-nUH*

any messages for me?
há algum recado para mim?
*ah ahl-**goom** RRae-**kah**-doo **pUH**-rUH meem?*

I would like to pay now, do you accept credit cards?
queria pagar, aceitam cartão de crédito?
*ke-**ree**-ya pUH-**gahr**, UH-**say**-tUHm kUHr-**toun** dae kreh-dee-too?*

I think there's a mistake in the bill
creio que há um erro na conta
kray-oo ke ah oom ae-RRoo nUH kon-tUH

Understanding

desculpe, estamos cheios/não temos nada livre
I'm sorry, but we're full

só temos disponível um quarto individual
we only have a single room available

para quantas noites?
how many nights is it for?

como se chama?
what's your name, please?

os quartos estão disponíveis a partir das 12h
check-in is from midday

tem de deixar o quarto (livre) antes das 11h
you have to check out before 11am

o pequeno-almoço é servido entre as 7h30 e as 9h
breakfast is served between 7.30 and 9.00

deseja um jornal pela manhã?
would you like a newspaper in the morning?

pode deixar a bagagem aqui
you can leave your bags here

o quarto ainda não está pronto
your room isn't ready yet

YOUTH HOSTELS

Expressing yourself

do you have space for two people for tonight?
tem lugar para duas pessoas para esta noite?
taim loo-gahr pUH-rUH doo-UHsh pe-so-UHsh pUH-rUH ehsh-tUH noy-t?

we've booked two beds for three nights
reservámos duas camas por três noites
RRae-zer-vah-moosh doo-UHsh kUH-mUHsh poor traysh noy-tesh

could I leave my backpack at reception?
posso deixar a minha mochila na recepção?
poh-soo day-shahr UH meen-ya moo-shee-lUH nUH RRae-sehp-soun?

do you have somewhere we could leave our bikes?
há algum sítio para deixar as bicicletas?
ah ahl-goom see-tee-yo pUH-rUH day-shahr UHsh bee-see-kleh-tUHsh?

I'll come back for it around 7 o'clock
virei buscá-la por volta das sete (horas)
vee-ray boosh-kah-lUH poor vohl-tUH dUHsh seh-t (oh-rUHsh)

there's no hot water
não há água quente
noun ah ah-gwUH kain-t

the sink's blocked
a pia está entupida
UH pee-ya esh-tah ain-too-pee-dUH

Understanding

cozinha de alberguista
cooking facilities/kitchen

pátio interior/exterior	beer garden, patio
quarto múltiplo	dormitory
sala de convívio	common room

tem cartão de membro?
do you have a membership card?

fornecemos lençóis
bed linen is provided

a pousada reabre às 18h
the hostel reopens at 6pm

SELF-CATERING

Expressing yourself

we're looking for somewhere to rent near town
queríamos alugar qualquer coisa perto da cidade
*ke-**ree**-yUH-moosh UH-loo-**gahr** kwahl-**kehr** koy-zUH **pehr**-too dUH see-dah-d*

where do we pick up/leave the keys?
onde obtemos/deixamos as chaves?
*on-d ohb-**tae**-moosh/day-**shUH**-moosh UHsh **shah**-vesh?*

is electricity included in the price?
a electricidade está incluída no preço?
*UH ee-leh-tree-see-**dah**-d esh-**tah** een-kloo-ee-dUH noo **prae**-soo?*

are bed linen and towels provided?
fornecem lençóis e toalhas?
*foor-**neh**-saim lain-**soh**-eesh ee too-**ahl**-yUHsh?*

is a car necessary?
é preciso carro?
*eh prae-**see**-zoo **kah**-RRoo?*

where is the pool?
onde é a piscina?
*on-d eh UH pee-**see**-nUH?*

is the accommodation suitable for elderly people?
o alojamento é adequado para pessoas idosas?
*oo UH-loo-JUH-**main**-too eh UH-dae-**kwah**-doo **pUH**-rUH pe-**so**-UHsh ee-**doh**-zUHsh?*

where is the nearest supermarket?
onde fica o supermercado mais perto?
*on-d **fee**-kUH oo soo-pehr-mer-**kah**-doo **my**-sh **pehr**-too?*

Understanding

por favor, deixar a casa limpa e arrumada
please leave the house clean and tidy when you leave

a casa está completamente mobilada
the house is fully furnished

está tudo incluído no preço
everything is included in the price

nesta parte do país precisa de carro
you really need a car in this part of the country

CAMPING

Expressing yourself

is there a campsite near here?
há algum parque de campismo aqui perto?
ah ahl-goom pahr-k dae kam-peesh-moo UH-kee pehr-too?

I'd like to book a space for a two-person tent for three nights
queria reservar um espaço para uma tenda dupla por três noites
ke-ree-ya RRae-zer-vahr oom esh-pah-soo pUH-rUH oo-mUH tain-dUH doo-plUH poor traysh noy-tesh

where is the shower block?
onde ficam os chuveiros?
on-d fee-kam oosh shoo-vay-roosh?

how much is it a night?
quanto custa por noite?
kwUHn-too koosh-tUH poor noy-t?

can we pay, please? we're at space …
queríamos pagar; estamos no número …
ke-ree-yUH-moosh pUH-gahr; esh-tUH-moosh noo noo-mae-roo …

Understanding

são … por pessoa, por noite
it's … per person per night

se precisar de alguma coisa, venha falar comigo
if you need anything, just come and ask

43

EATING AND DRINKING

Portugal offers a wide choice of restaurants. **Tascas** are small, inexpensive places popular with locals. **Casas de pasto** are a bit bigger and serve simple food at reasonable prices. Proper restaurants tend to be smarter with a more varied menu. **Marisqueiras**, usually found on the coast, specialize in fish and seafood while **churrasqueiras** serve grilled meat. Another option is a **cervejaria** (brasserie), which serves light meals and, of course, beer.

Service is not included in most restaurants, and you should leave a tip – around ten per cent of the total bill is standard.

A typical Portuguese lunch or dinner might start with soup, followed by a fish or meat dish with potatoes and rice, and a dessert. The dish of the day is often a local speciality. You'll be served an appetizer when you sit down (cheese, ham, chorizo sausage, olives, tuna paté etc), but will only be charged for it if you eat it. One portion (**dose**) is often enough for two people, and it's sometimes possible to order a half-portion (**meia-dose**). Water is not provided automatically; you will have to order it, specifying whether you would like still or sparkling.

If you want to go for a drink you can go to a **tasca** or **cervejaria**, or try one of the cafés or **pastelarias** (cake shops) so popular in Portugal. These may also serve sandwiches and snacks. Cafés are lively, sociable places, and people often come in after going for a meal. On summer evenings, you can relax on the terrace for as long as you like (though prices are generally higher if you sit outside). In cities, people tend to move from one bar to another. There is a wide variety of bottled beers and **fino** (draft beer) available. The legal drinking age is 16.

The basics

beer	cerveja *ser-vae-JUH*
bill	conta *kon-tUH*

black coffee	bica *bee-kUH*, café *kUH-feh*
bottle	garrafa *gUH-RRah-fUH*
bread	pão *pouŋ*
breakfast	pequeno-almoço *pe-kae-noo ahl-mo-soo*
cake	bolo *bo-loo*
coffee	café *kUH-feh*
Coke®	Coca-cola® *koh-kUH koh-lUH*
dessert	sobremesa *so-bre-mae-zUH*
dinner	jantar *JUHn-tahr*
espresso	bica *bee-kUHJ*, café *kUH-feh*
fruit juice	sumo *soo-moo*
lemonade	gasosa *gUH-zoh-zUH*
lunch	almoço *ahl-mo-soo*
main course	prato principal *prah-too preen-see-pahl*
menu	menu *meh-noo*, ementa *ee-main-tUH*
mineral water	água mineral *ah-gwUH mee-ne-rahl*
red wine	vinho tinto *veen-yoo teen-too*
rosé wine	vinho rosé *veen-yoo roh-zae*
salad	salada *sUH-lah-dUH*
sandwich	sandes *sUHn-desh*, sanduíche *sUHn-doo-eesh*
service	serviço *ser-vee-soo*
sparkling	*(wine)* espumante *esh-poo-mUHn-t*; *(water)* com gás *kom gahsh*
starter	entrada *ain-trah-dUH*
still	*(water)* sem gás *saim gahsh*
tea	chá *shah*
tip	gorgeta *goor-Jae-tUH*
water	água *ah-gwUH*
white coffee	meia-de-leite *may-UH dae lay-t*
white wine	vinho branco *veen-yoo brUHn-koo*
wine	vinho *veen-yoo*
wine list	lista de vinhos *leesh-tUH dae veen-yoosh*
to drink	beber *bae-baer*
to eat	comer *koo-maer*
to have breakfast	tomar o pequeno-almoço *to-mahr oo pe-kae-noo ahl-mo-soo*
to have dinner	jantar *JUHn-tahr*
to have lunch	almoçar *ahl-moo-sahr*
to order	pedir *pe-deer*

Expressing yourself

shall we go and have something to eat?
vamos comer qualquer coisa?
vUH-moosh koo-maer kwahl-kehr koy-zUH?

do you want to go for a drink?
vamos beber um copo?
vUH-moosh bae-baer oom koh-poo?

can you recommend a good restaurant?
aconselha-me um bom restaurante?
UH-kon-sael-yUH-mae oom bom RResh-tow-rUHn-t?

I'm not very hungry
não tenho muita fome
noun tain-yoo mooy-tUH foh-m

I'm very hungry
estou cheio/cheia de fome
esh-to shay-oo/shay-UH dae foh-m

do you have a table for three people?
tem uma mesa para três pessoas?
taim oo-mUH mae-zUH pUH-rUH traysh pe-so-UHsh?

excuse me! *(to call the waiter)*
se faz favor!
s-fahsh fUH-vor!

could you bring me a menu?
posso ver a ementa?
poh-soo vaer UH ee-main-tUH?

cheers!
saúde!
sUH-oo-d!

that was lovely
estava óptimo/óptima
esh-tah-vUH oh-tee-moo/oh-tee-mUH

could you bring us an ashtray, please?
(podia trazer-nos) um cinzeiro, se faz favor?
(po-dee-ya trah-zaer-noosh) oom seen-zay-roo, s-fahsh fUH-vor?

where are the toilets, please?
onde são as casas-de-banho?
on-d soun ash kah-zUHsh dae bUHn-yoo?

Understanding

ao quilo	by weight
para levar	takeaway
pré-pagamento	prepayment

EATING AND DRINKING

lamento, mas depois das onze (horas) já não servimos
I'm sorry, we stop serving at 11pm

RESERVING A TABLE

Expressing yourself

I'd like to book a table for tomorrow evening
gostaria de reservar uma mesa para amanhã à noite
goosh-tUH-__ree__-ya dae RRae-zer-__vahr__ oo-mUH mae-zUH pUH-rUH ah-mUHn-yUH ah __noy__-t

for two people
para duas pessoas
pUH-rUH doo-UHsh pe-so-UHsh

around 8 o'clock
para as oito (horas)
pUH-rUH ash oy-too (oh-rUHsh)

do you have a table available any earlier than that?
tem alguma mesa disponível mais cedo?
taim ahl-__goo__-mUH mae-zUH deesh-poo-__nee__-vehl my-sh __sae__-doo?

I've reserved a table – the name's ...
reservei uma mesa, o nome é ...
RRae-zer-__vay__ oo-mUH mae-zUH, oo __no__-m eh ...

Understanding

reservado
reserved

para que horas?
for what time?

para quantas pessoas?
for how many people?

qual é o nome?
what's the name?

fumadores ou não fumadores?
smoking or non-smoking?

fez reserva?/tem mesa reservada?
do you have a reservation?

esta mesa, aqui no canto, está bem?
is this table in the corner OK for you?

estamos cheios, mas se quiser esperar um pouco verei o que posso fazer
I'm afraid we're full at the moment, but if you don't mind waiting a while, I'll see what I can do

47

ORDERING FOOD

Expressing yourself

yes, we're ready to order
sim, creio que já escolhemos
seeŋ, kray-oo ke Jah esh-kool-yae-moosh

no, could you give us a few more minutes?
ainda não, pode dar-nos mais uns minutos?
UH-een-dUH nouŋ, poh-d dahr-noosh my-sh oonsh mee-noo-toosh?

I'd like …
queria …
ke-ree-ya …

what do you recommend?
o que é que recomenda?
oo ke eh ke RRe-koo-main-dUH?

I'm not sure, what's "açorda"?
não tenho a certeza, o que é "açorda"?
nouŋ tain-yoo UH saer-tae-zUH, oo ke eh UH-sor-dUH?

I'll have that
pode ser isso então
poh-d saer ee-soo ain-touŋ

what does it come with?
é servido com quê?
eh saer-vee-doo kom kae?

what are today's specials?
quais são os pratos do dia?
kwah-eesh souŋ oosh prah-toosh do dee-ya?

what desserts do you have?
que sobremesas tem?
ke so-bre-mae-zUHsh taim?

some water, please
água, se faz favor
ah-gwUH, s-fahsh fUH-vor

a bottle of red/white wine
uma garrafa de vinho tinto/branco
oo-mUH gUH-RRah-fUH dae veen-yoo teen-too/brUHn-koo

that's for me
para mim
pUH-rUH meem

this isn't what I ordered, I wanted …
não é o que eu pedi, eu queria …
nouŋ eh oo ke ae-oo pae-dee, ae-oo ke-ree-ya …

could we have some more bread, please?
(podia trazer-nos) mais pão, se faz favor?
*(po-**dee**-ya trUH-**zaer**-noosh) my-sh pouŋ, s-fahsh fUH-vor?*

could you bring us another jug of water, please?
(podia trazer-nos) mais uma jarra de água, se faz favor?
*(po-**dee**-ya trUH-**zaer**-noosh) my-sh oo-mUH Jah-RRUH dah-gwUH, s-fahsh
fUH-vor?*

Understanding

já escolheu/escolheram?
are you ready to order?

então, volto mais tarde
I'll come back in a few minutes

o que é que vai/vão beber?
what would you like to drink?

lamento, mas já não temos ...
I'm sorry, we don't have any ... left

está tudo bem?
is everything OK?

vai/vão querer sobremesa ou café?
would you like dessert or coffee?

BARS AND CAFÉS

Expressing yourself

I'd like...
queria...
*ke-**ree**-ya...*

a black/white coffee
um café/um café com leite
*oom kUH-**feh**/oom kUH-**feh** kom lay-t*

a Coke®/a diet Coke®
uma Coca-cola®/ uma Coca-cola® light
oo-mUH koh-kUH koh-lUH/oo-mUH koh-kUH koh-lUH light

a glass of white/red wine
um copo de vinho branco/tinto
oom koh-poo dae veen-yoo brUHn-koo/teen-too

a cup of tea
uma chávena de chá
oo-mUH shah-ve-nUH dae shah

a coffee and a croissant
um café e um croissant
oom kUH-feh ee oom kroo-ah-sUHn

the same again, please
o mesmo, se faz favor
oo maysh-moo, s-fahsh fUH-vor

a cup of hot chocolate
um chocolate quente
oom shoo-koo-lah-t kain-t

Understanding

à mesa	at the table
ao balcão	at the bar
na esplanada	outside
sem álcool	non-alcoholic

não pode/podem fumar aqui
this is a non-smoking area

o que é que vai/vão querer/tomar?
what would you like?

importa-se/importam-se de pagar agora, se faz favor?
could I ask you to pay now, please?

> **Some informal expressions**
>
> **estar com os copos** to be drunk
> **estar com ressaca** to have a hangover

THE BILL

Expressing yourself

the bill, please
a conta, se faz favor
UH kon-tUH, s-fahsh fUH-vor

how much do I owe you?
quanto devo?
kwUHn-too dae-voo?

do you take credit cards?
aceita cartão de crédito?
UH-say-tUH kUHr-toun dae kreh-dee-too?

keep the change
guarde o troco
gwahr-d oo tro-koo

is service included?
o serviço está incluído?
oo ser-vee-soo esh-tah een-kloo-ee-doo?

Understanding

tudo junto ou separado?
are you all paying together?

sim, inclui o serviço
yes, service is included

FOOD AND DRINK

Portuguese cuisine uses lots of olive oil and is richly flavoured with herbs (rosemary, bay leaves etc). Rice is more popular than vegetables, and is served with almost every meal. There is a wide variety of desserts, many of them featuring eggs.

If you like fish and seafood you should head for the coast. Prices are generally quite reasonable and portions are generous. Many restaurants offer a set menu for tourists, comprising two or three courses, a drink and coffee.

Understanding

ao vapor	steamed
às fatias/às rodelas	sliced
(assado) na brasa	chargrilled, charcoal grilled
assado no forno	roasted; baked
bem-passado	well done
corado	browned
cozido	boiled
de cebolada/de escabeche	with a fried onion sauce
derretido	melted
dourado	browned
estufado	slowly stewed
fatiado	sliced
fresco	fresh
frio	cold
frito	fried
fumado	smoked
gratinado	au gratin
grelhado	grilled
guisado	stewed
mal-passado	rare
marinado	marinated

no churrasco	barbecued, grilled
no espeto	on the spit
no ponto	just right
panado	breaded
recheado	stuffed
refogado	stewed
salteado	sautéed
seco	dried
temperado	seasoned, dressed

◆ pequenos-almoços e lanches breakfasts and snacks

açúcar	sugar
arrufada	sweet bun
bolacha	biscuit
bolo	cake
bolo de arroz	small cake made with rice flour
bica	espresso
bica cheia	double espresso
café	coffee, espresso
café com leite	white coffee
carioca	small instant coffee
carioca de limão	fresh lemon rind infusion
cereais	cereals
chá	tea
chá de camomila	camomile tea
chá preto/verde	black/green tea
chocolate quente	hot chocolate
cimbalino	espresso
compota	preserve
coxinha de galinha	chicken rissole *(shaped like a drumstick)*
croissant	croissant
descafeinado	decaffeinated espresso
doce	
empada	pasty, small pie
empada de galinha	chicken pasty/pie
galão	large white coffee
garoto	espresso with a drop of milk
geleia	jam

iogurte	yoghurt
leite	milk
manteiga	butter
margarina	margarine
marmelada	quince jelly
meia-de-leite	regular white coffee
mel	honey
panado no pão	breaded pork steak in a roll
pão	bread
pão-de-leite	brioche
pastel de carne	sausage roll, meat pasty
pingo	espresso with a drop of milk
prego	small pork steak sandwich/roll
queijo	cheese
requeijão	cottage cheese
sandes/sanduíche	sandwich
sumo de laranja natural	fresh orange juice
sumo (de fruta)	(fruit) juice
torradas	toast
tosta	toasted sandwich
tosta mista	cheese and ham toasted sandwich

◆ **aperitivos, sopas e entradas** appetizers, soups and starters

açorda	bread soup seasoned with lots of garlic and coriander
azeitonas	olives
broa (de milho)	corn bread
caldo verde	soup made with potatoes, greens and cured sausage
camarão	prawns; shrimps
canja de galinha	chicken broth
caracóis	snails
chouriça/chouriço	cured pork sausage
creme de cenoura	carrot soup
creme de marisco	seafood soup
croquetes	croquettes
enchidos	different types of cured sausages

esparregado	creamed spinach
linguiça	thin cured pork sausage
meia desfeita	chickpea salad
melão com presunto	melon with ham
moelas	chicken giblets
pão e manteiga	bread and butter
pasta de atum	tuna paté
pasta de queijo	cheese spread
pasta de sardinha	sardine paté
pastéis de bacalhau	deep fried salt cod and potato cakes
paté de atum	tuna paté
paté de sardinha	sardine paté
pickles	pickles
pipis	chicken giblets
presunto	cured ham
queijo	cheese
queijinhos saloios	typical small cheeses *(made of goat's or sheep's milk or a mixture)*
queijo fresco	fresh cheese *(ricotta type)*
rissóis de camarão	shrimp rissoles
rissóis de carne/de pescada	meat/hake rissoles
salada de alface	green salad *(lettuce only)*
salada de feijão-frade	black-eyed bean salad
salada mista	mixed salad *(usually lettuce, tomatoes and onion)*
salada russa	potato salad
sopa de abóbora	pumpkin soup
sopa de agrião	watercress soup
sopa de feijão verde	green bean soup
sopa de grão	chickpea soup
sopa de hortaliça	cabbage and bean soup
sopa de legumes	vegetable soup
sopa de pedra	minestrone *(meat, bean and pasta soup)*
sopa de peixe	fish soup

◆ pratos principais main courses

Bacalhau (salt cod) is without a doubt Portugal's favourite fish: there are said to be 365 different ways of cooking it!

Sardines are popular too, and are traditionally served at St John's day village celebrations (24 June). Seafood and shellfish also feature in many dishes.

◆ peixe, crustáceos e marisco fish, shellfish and seafood

arroz de lampreia	lamprey *(type of eel)* rice
arroz de marisco	seafood rice
arroz de polvo	octopus rice
arroz de tamboril	monkfish rice
bacalhau à Brás	salt cod with thin French fries, onions, eggs, garlic, olives and parsley
bacalhau à Lagareiro	breaded salt cod cooked in olive oil, garlic and milk
bacalhau à Gomes de Sá	salt cod with potatoes, onions, boiled eggs, garlic, olives and parsley
bacalhau à Zé do Pipo	baked salt cod with onions, mashed potatoes, mayonnaise and olives
bacalhau (assado) no forno	baked salt cod, usually with onion, tomatoes and peppers
bacalhau com natas	baked salt cod with potatoes, onions and cream
bacalhau na brasa	chargrilled salt cod
bacalhau podre	salt cod in batter in a tomato, onion and egg sauce
caldeirada de peixe	fish stew, chowder
carapau grelhado	grilled scad
carapaus de escabeche	fried scad served with an onion and vinegar sauce
cataplana	fish and seafood cooked in a fish kettle
cherne grelhado	grilled grouper
chocos com tinta	cuttlefish cooked in ink
dourada grelhada	grilled dorado
feijoada de gambas	bean and prawn stew

feijoada de marisco	bean and seafood stew
feijoada de polvo	bean and octopus stew
filetes de pescada	hake fillets in batter
linguado grelhado	grilled sole
lulas grelhadas	grilled squid
lulas recheadas	stuffed squid
migas de bacalhau	shredded salt cod mixed with bread, garlic, olive oil and herbs
pataniscas	salt cod pieces fried in batter
pescada com todos	boiled hake with potatoes, eggs and green beans
polvo grelhado	grilled octopus
robalo grelhado	grilled sea bass
santola (recheada)	stuffed crab
sardinhas assadas	grilled sardines

◆ carne e aves meat and poultry

almôndegas	meatballs
arroz à valenciana	rice with chicken and seafood
arroz de cabidela	rice with chicken and chicken blood
arroz de pato	rice with duck and cured sausage cooked in the oven
bifanas	fried wine-marinated pork steaks
bife	(beef)steak
bife de alcatra	rump steak
bitoque	steak served with a fried egg on top, garnished with chips and salad
bucho	roast pork stomach stuffed with rice and meat
cabrito assado	roast kid goat
carne de porco à alentejana	pork cooked with clams
chanfana	goat's meat cooked in red wine
chispalhada	bean and vegetable stew with pig's trotters, pig's ear and cured sausage
coelho à caçadora	rabbit stew
cozido à portuguesa	mixed boiled meats (beef, chicken, pork), cured sausages (black pudding etc) and vegetables served with rice
dobrada	tripe cooked with pork and white beans

ensopado de borrego	stewed lamb on a bed of bread
entrecosto	spare ribs
entremeada grelhada	grilled pork belly
escalopes de peru	turkey escalopes
favas à portuguesa	broad bean stew with cured sausage and bacon
feijoada	bean and pork stew
frango de cabidela	chicken with rice and chicken blood
frango na púcara	chicken stewed in wine in a special earthenware pot
jardineira	meat and mixed vegetable stew
iscas de fígado	fried marinated slivers of liver
leitão assado/leitão da Bairrada	roast suckling pig
lombo (de porco assado)	roast pork loin
negalhos	small parcels of lamb tripe cooked in red wine
pernil/perna de borrego	leg of lamb
rojões à moda do Minho	fried marinated pork pieces
tripas à moda do Porto	tripe cooked with veal and white beans

◆ **sobremesas** desserts

There are some excellent cheeses to be found in Portugal, such as the famous **Queijo da Serra** (from Serra da Estrela) and **Queijo da Ilha** (from the Azores).

Many Portuguese desserts are based on traditional convent recipes, such as **Toucinho do Céu** (which translates as "bacon from heaven", but is actually a baked egg custard flavoured with almonds), **Barrigas de Freira** (dessert of egg yolks, syrup and bread) and **Queijadas de Sintra** (a type of small cheesecake).

aletria	vermicelli dessert
arroz doce	rice pudding

baba de camelo	eggs and condensed milk dessert
bolo de bolacha	biscuit, coffee and cream dessert
bolo inglês	fruit cake
bolo podre	molasses and almond cake
broas de mel	sweet bread made from cornflour, honey and olive oil
farófias	dessert made with egg whites, milk, cinnamon and custard
fios de ovos	egg yolk filaments cooked in syrup
gelado	ice cream
leite-creme	similar to créme brûlée
Molotof	light, spongy pudding made with egg whites and caramel
mousse de chocolate	chocolate mousse
ovos moles	very sweet sauce made with egg yolks and syrup
pão-de-ló	sponge cake
papos de anjo	small pastries made with syrup, jam, eggs and cinnamon
pastéis de nata	custard tarts
pastéis de feijão	sweet bean pastries
pastéis de Tentúgal	long thin filo pastries with an egg yolk and syrup filling
pudim flan	crème caramel
salada de frutas	fruit salad
sorbete	sorbet
tarte de queijo	cheesecake

FOOD AND DRINK GLOSSARY

abacate avocado
abóbora pumpkin
açafrão saffron
ácido/a acidic
acompanhamento garnish
adoçante sweetener
agrião watercress
agridoce sweet and sour
água mineral mineral water

aguardente velha brandy
água tónica tonic water
aipo celery
alcachofra artichoke
alcaparras capers
alface lettuce
alecrim rosemary
alheira sausage made from white meat, bread and spices

alho garlic
alho francês leek
alperce apricot
amêijoas clams
ameixa plum
amêndoa amarga bitter almond liqueur
amêndoas almonds
amêndoas salgadas salted almonds
amendoins peanuts
amoras blackberries
ananás pineapple
anchovas anchovies
aperitivo aperitif
aquecer to heat up
arenque herring
arenque fumado kipper
arroz rice
arroz branco plain rice
assado roast
assar to roast; to bake
atum tuna
avelãs hazelnuts
azeite olive oil
bacalhau (salgado) salt cod
bacon bacon
badejo pollack
bagaço strong clear spirit
banana banana
banha lard
batatas potatoes
batatas a murro small baked potatoes
batatas fritas chips; crisps
batido milkshake
bebida drink
berbigão cockles
beringela aubergine

besugo sea bream
beterraba beetroot
bife de atum tuna steak
biscoito biscuit, cookie
bola de carne bread stuffed with meat
borrego lamb
brócolos broccoli
caça game
cação dogfish
cacau cocoa
cachorro quente hot dog
cajus cashew nuts
calda syrup
caldo stock
caneca *(beer)* half-litre measure of beer
canela cinnamon
caranguejo crab
carne de porco pork
carne de vaca beef
carneiro mutton
carne picada minced meat
carnes frias cold meats
caseiro/a homemade
castanhas chestnuts
cavala mackerel
cebola onion
cebolinho chives
cenoura carrot
cerejas cherries
cerveja beer
cerveja preta stout
chocolate chocolate
chocolate branco/preto white/ dark chocolate
chocolate de leite milk chocolate
chocos cuttlefish
cidra cider

clara de ovo egg white
coco coconut
codorniz quail
coentros coriander
cogumelos mushrooms
colorau paprika
comida food
cominhos cumin
congelado/a frozen
congro conger eel
conservante preservative
copo glass
coração heart
cordeiro lamb
cortar to cut, to chop
cortar aos palitos to cut in strips
cortar aos quadrados to dice
corvina black bream
costeleta chop
couve cabbage
couve de Bruxelas brussel
 sprouts
couve-flor cauliflower
couve galega type of kale
couve lombarda savoy cabbage
couve serrana type of kale
coxa de frango drumstick
cozido/a boiled
cozinhar to cook
cravinho cloves
cru(a) raw
crustáceos shellfish
de conserva tinned
dente de alho clove of garlic
desossado/a boned
doce sweet
duro/a *(bread)* stale, old; *(meat)*
 tough
em lata tinned

eirós elvers
enguia eel
erva-doce aniseed
ervilhas peas
espadarte swordfish
espargos asparagus
esparguete spaghetti
especiarias spices
espesso/a thick
espetada skewer, kebab
espinafres spinach
espinha fishbone
estragão tarragon
farinha flour
farinheira sausage made with
 flour, pork fat, paprika and herbs
favas broad beans
febras (de porco) pork fillets
fécula potato starch
feijão branco white beans; butter
 beans
feijão encarnado kidney beans
feijão preto black beans
fígado liver
figo fig
filete fillet
fino schooner of beer
flocos de aveia porridge oats
flocos de milho cornflakes
folha de louro bayleaf
forno oven
forno de lenha wood oven
framboesas raspberries
frango chicken
frango churrasco barbecued
 chicken
fritar to fry
fruta fruit
fruta da época fruit in season

funcho fennel
galinha chicken
gambas large prawns
ganso goose
gelo ice
gema de ovo egg yolk
gengibre ginger
ginginha cherry brandy
girafa *(beer)* litre tankard of beer
grão chickpeas
grelos turnip or cabbage shoots
groselhas redcurrants
guarnição garnish
hortelã mint
imperial schooner of beer
ingredientes ingredients
inteiro/a whole
javali wild boar
lagosta lobster
lagostins crayfish
laranja orange
lata tin, can
lavagante lobster
lebre hare
legumes vegetables
leite milk
leite gordo whole milk
leite magro skimmed milk
leite meio-gordo semi-skimmed milk
lentilhas lentils
lima lime
limão lemon
louro bayleaf
lúcio pike
maçã apple
maçã assada baked apple
maduro/a ripe
maionese mayonnaise

malagueta chilli pepper
manjericão basil
marisco seafood
marmelo quince
massa pasta; dough
massa folhada puff pastry
medalhão medallion
melancia watermelon
meloa cantaloupe melon
menta mint
mexilhões mussels
migalhas crumbs
milho corn
milho (doce) sweetcorn
molho sauce
morango strawberry
morcela black pudding
mostarda mustard
nabiça turnip greens
nabo turnip
natas cream
nectarina nectarine
novilho beef
nozes walnuts
noz moscada nutmeg
óleo cooking oil
omelete omelette
orégãos oregano
osso bone
ostras oysters
ovas fish roe
ovo egg
ovo cozido/duro hard-boiled egg
ovo escalfado poached egg
ovo estrelado fried egg
ovo quente soft boiled egg
ovos mexidos scrambled eggs
paio lean cured pork sausage
pão bread; roll

pão de centeio rye bread
pão de forma sandwich loaf
pão integral wholemeal bread
papo-seco roll
pargo sea bream
passa raisin
pastel small cake
pato duck
peixe-espada scabbard fish
pepino cucumber
pêra pear
perdiz partridge
pêssego peach
pêssego careca/pelado nectarine
petinga small sardines
picante hot, spicy
pimenta pepper
pimenta em grão peppercorns
pimentão-doce paprika
pimento verde green pepper
pinhões pine nuts
pipocas popcorn
piri-piri chilli pepper; chilli sauce
prato dish; plate
pudim pudding
puré mashed potatoes
rabanadas French toast
rabanete radish
raia skate
refrigerante soft drink
rim kidney
rodovalho turbot
rosmaninho rosemary

safio small conger eel
sal salt
salchicha sausage
salgadinho savoury snack
salgado/a salted
salmão salmon
salmonete red mullet
salpicão type of cured pork sausage
salsa parsley
santola spider crab
sementes seeds
solha plaice
tamboril monkfish
tangerina tangerine
temperar to season, to dress
tempero seasoning, dressing
tenro/a tender
tomate tomato
tomilho thyme
toucinho streaky bacon
tremoços lupini beans
truta trout
uvas grapes
vieiras scallops
vinagre vinegar
vinho wine
vinho da casa house wine
vinho de mesa table wine
vinho do Porto port
vinho moscatel Muscatel wine
vinho verde light, slightly sparkling white wine
vitela veal

You can find out about cultural events in tourist information offices. Some also sell tickets for shows and concerts. In Lisbon and other big cities, there is a free monthly listings magazine called **Agenda Cultural** available in tourist information centres, hotels, newspaper kiosks and so on.

Going to the cinema is cheap and is one of the most popular pastimes in Portugal. Most cinemas offer discounts on Mondays.

Eating and drinking are big social events. If you are invited to somebody's house, take a bottle of wine or a dessert as a gift for your host and don't be too punctual. The Portuguese tend to go out quite late; clubs and discos don't fill up until midnight or 1am. Admission usually includes a free drink.

The basics

ballet	bailado *bah-ee-lah-doo*
band	banda *bUHn-dUH,* conjunto *kon-Joon-too*
bar	bar *bar*
cinema	cinema *see-nae-mUH*
circus	circo *seer-koo*
classical music	música clássica *moo-zee-kUH klah-see-kUH*
club	discoteca *deesh-koo-teh-kUH*
concert	concerto *kon-saer-too*
funfair	feira popular *fay-rUH poo-poo-lahr*
festival	festival *fesh-tee-vahl*
film	filme *feel-m*
folk music	música popular *moo-zee-kUH poo-poo-lahr*
group	grupo *groo-poo*
jazz	jazz *Jah-z*
modern dance	dança moderna *dUHn-sUH moo-dehr-nUH*
musical	musical *moo-zee-kahl*
party	festa *fehsh-tUH*
play	peça (de teatro) *peh-sUH (dae te-ah-troo)*
pop music	música pop *moo-zee-kUH poh-p*
rock music	(música) rock *(moo-zee-kUH) RRoh-k*

show	espectáculo *esh-peh-tah-koo-loo*
subtitled film	filme com legendas *feel-m kom le-Jain-dUHsh*
theatre	teatro *te-ah-troo*
ticket	bilhete *beel-yae-t*
to book	reservar *RRae-zer-vahr*
to go out	sair *sUH-eer*

SUGGESTIONS AND INVITATIONS

Expressing yourself

where can we go?
onde podemos ir?
on-d poo-dae-moosh eer?

what do you want to do?
o que é que quer/querem fazer?
oo ke eh ke kehr/keh-raim fUH-zaer?

shall we go for a drink?
vamos tomar um copo?
vUH-moosh too-mahr oom koh-poo?

what are you doing tonight?
o que é que vai/vão fazer hoje à noite?
oo ke eh ke vaee/voun fUH-zaer o-Je ah noy-t?

do you have plans?
já tem/têm planos?
Jah taim/tae-aim plUH-noosh?

would you like to ...?
quer/querem ...?
kehr/keh-raim ...?

we were thinking of going to ...
estávamos a pensar ir a ...
esh-tah-vUH-moosh UH pain-sahr eer UH ...

I can't today, but maybe some other time
hoje não posso, mas talvez outro dia
o-Je noun poh-soo, mUHsh tahl-vaysh o-troo dee-ya

I'm not sure I can make it
não sei se poderei ir
noun say se poo-de-ray eer

I'd love to
adorava ir
UH-doo-rah-vUH eer

ARRANGING TO MEET

Expressing yourself

what time shall we meet?
a que horas nos encontramos?
UH ke oh-rUHsh noosh ain-kon-trUH-moosh?

where shall we meet?
onde nos encontramos?
on-d noosh ain-kon-trUH-moosh?

would it be possible to meet a bit later?
podia ser um pouco mais tarde?
poo-dee-ya saer oom po-koo my-sh tahr-d?

I have to meet … at nine
tenho um encontro marcado com… às nove
taen-yo oom ain-kon-troo mUHr-kah-doo kom… ash noh-v

I don't know where it is but I'll find it on the map
não sei onde é, mas vejo no mapa
noun say on-d eh, mUHsh vae-Joo noo mah-pUH

see you tomorrow night
então, até amanhã (à noite)
ain-toun, UH-teh ah-mUHn-yUH (ah noy-t)

I'll meet you later, I have to stop by the hotel first
até mais tarde, tenho primeiro que passar pelo hotel
UH-teh my-sh tahr-d, tain-yo pree-may-roo ke pUH-sahr pae-loo oh-tehl

I'll call/text you if there's a change of plan
eu telefono/envio uma mensagem se houver alguma mudança de planos
ae-oo te-le-foh-noo/ain-vee-oo oo-mUH main-sah-Jaim see oh-vehr ahl-goo-mUH moo-dUHn-sUH dae plUH-noosh

are you going to eat beforehand?
comes alguma coisa antes?
koo-maesh ahl-goo-mUH koy-zUH UHn-tesh?

sorry I'm late
peço desculpa pelo atraso
peh-soo desh-kool-pUH pae-loo UH-trah-zoo

GOING OUT

Understanding

está bem?
is that ok with you?

venho buscá-lo/buscá-la às oito
I'll come and pick you up about 8

encontro-o/encontro-a/encontro-vos lá
I'll meet you there

podemos encontrar-nos cá fora
we can meet outside

vou dar-lhe o meu número e pode telefonar-me amanhã
I'll give you my number and you can call me tomorrow

> **Some informal expressions**
>
> **ir comer qualquer coisa** to go out for a bite to eat
> **ir dar uma volta** to go for a walk/a drive
> **ir tomar um copo** to go for a drink

FILMS, SHOWS AND CONCERTS

Expressing yourself

is there a guide to what's on?
há algum guia de espectáculos?
ah ahl-goom gee-ya desh-peh-tah-koo-loosh?

I'd like three tickets for ...
queria três bilhetes para ...
ke-ree-ya traysh beel-yae-tesh pUH-rUH ...

two tickets, please
dois bilhetes, se faz favor
doy-eesh beel-yae-tesh, s-fahsh fUH-vor

it's called ...
chama-se ...
shUH-mUH-se ...

I've seen the trailer
ví a apresentação
vee UH UH-pre-sain-tUH-souη

what time does it start?
a que horas começa?
*UH ke **oh**-rUHsh koo-**meh**-sUH?*

I'd like to go and see a show
gostava de ir ver um espectáculo
*goosh-**tah**-vUH dae eer vaer oom esh-peh-**tah**-koo-loo*

I'll find out whether there are still tickets available
vou ver se ainda há bilhetes
*vo vaer se UH-**een**-dUH ah beel-**yae**-tesh*

do we need to book in advance?
é preciso reservar antes?
*eh pre-**see**-zoo RRae-zer-**vahr** UHn-tesh?*

how long is it on for?
até quando é que vai estar?
*UH-**teh** kwUHn-doo eh ke **vah**-ee esh-**tahr**?*

are there tickets for another day?
há bilhetes para outro dia?
*ah beel-**yae**-tesh p**UH**-rUH o-troo **dee**-ya?*

I'd like to go to a bar with some live music
gostava de ir a um bar com música ao vivo
*goosh-**tah**-vUH dae eer UH oom bar kom **moo**-zee-kUH ow **vee**-voo*

are there any free concerts?
há algum concerto que seja de graça?
*ah ahl-**goom** kon-**saer**-too ke sae-JUH dae grah-sUH?*

what sort of music is it?
que género de música é?
*ke Jeh-ne-roo dae **moo**-zee-kUH eh?*

Understanding

auditório	concert hall
bilheteira	box office
cinemateca	filmhouse
em exibição a partir de …	on general release from …
estreias	openings
lotação esgotada	sold out
(lugar com) visibilidade reduzida	restricted view

reservas	bookings
sala de espectáculos	concert hall/theatre
sessão	showing
teatro de variedades/de revista	revue

é um concerto ao ar livre
it's an open-air concert

teve muito boas críticas
it's had very good reviews

estreia na próxima semana
it comes out next week

começa às oito no Monumental
it's on at 8pm at the Monumental

essa sessão está esgotada
that showing's sold out

está esgotado até …
it's all booked up until …

não é preciso reservar
there's no need to book in advance

a peça dura uma hora e meia com o intervalo
the play lasts an hour and a half, including the interval

é favor de desligar os telemóveis
please turn off your mobile phones

PARTIES AND CLUBS

Expressing yourself

I'm having a little leaving party tonight
vou dar uma festa de despedida hoje à noite
*vo dahr **oo**-mUH **fehsh**-tUH dae desh-pe-**dee**-dUH o-Je ah **noy**-t*

should I bring something to drink?
levo alguma coisa para beber?
*leh-voo ahl-**goo**-mUH koy-zUH p**UH**-rUH bae-**baer**?*

we could go to a club afterwards
depois podíamos ir a uma discoteca
*de-**poy**-eesh po-**dee**-UH-moosh eer UH **oo**-mUH deesh-koo-**teh**-kUH*

do you have to pay to get in?
é preciso pagar para entrar?
*eh prae-**see**-zoo p**UH**-**gahr** p**UH**-rUH ain-**trahr**?*

I have to meet someone inside
marquei encontro com alguém lá dentro
*mUH-**kay** ain-**kon**-troo kom ahl-**gaim** lah **dain**-troo*

will you let me back in when I come back?
deixa-me entrar quando eu voltar?
*day-shUH-mae ain-**trahr** kwUHn-doo ae-oo vohl-**tahr**?*

the DJ's really cool
o DJ é mesmo bom
*oo dee-**Jay** eh **maysh**-moo bom*

do you come here often?
vem aqui muitas vezes?
*vaim UH-**kee** mooy-tUHsh **vae**-zesh?*

can I buy you a drink?
posso pagar-lhe uma bebida?
*poh-soo pUH-**gahr**-lyee oo-mUH bae-**bee**-dUH?*

thanks, but I'm with my boyfriend
não obrigado/obrigada, estou com o meu namorado
*noun o-bree-**gah**-doo/o-bree-**gah**-dUH, esh-**to** kom oo **mae**-oo nUH-moo-rah-doo*

no thanks, I don't smoke
não obrigado/obrigada, não fumo
*noun o-bree-**gah**-doo/o-bree-**gah**-dUH, noun **foo**-moo*

Understanding

bebida grátis
free drink

vestiário
cloakroom

15 euros depois da meia-noite
15 euros after midnight

há festa na casa do Armando
there's a party at Armando's place

quer dançar?
do you want to dance?

posso comprar-lhe uma bebida?
can I buy you a drink?

tem lume?
have you got a light?

tem um cigarro?
have you got a cigarette?

podemos nos ver outra vez?
can we see each other again?

posso levá-lo/levá-la a casa?
can I see you home?

GOING OUT

TOURISM AND SIGHTSEEING

All large Portuguese towns have a tourist information office where visitors can get local information, maps (usually free) and details of regional events and guided tours. They also provide useful information on hotels. Opening hours vary depending on the region, but they are generally the same as the local shops. In rural areas, tourist information offices may even close at weekends. Tourist information can also be found in large airports and in Portuguese tourist centres in other countries.

In general, museums are open from 10am until 5 or 6pm (closing for lunch from 12 or 12.30 to 2.30 or 3pm), from Tuesday to Sunday; most of them are closed on Mondays and bank holidays. Most museums charge an admission fee, but on Sundays, bank holidays and in the morning prices are often reduced and admission may even be free.

The basics

ancient	antigo/antiga *UHn-**tee**-goo/UHn-**tee**-gUH*
antique	antiguidade *UHn-tee-gwee-**dah**-d*
area	zona *zo-nUH*
castle	castelo *kUHsh-**teh**-loo*
cathedral	catedral *kUH-tae-**drahl***
century	século *seh-koo-loo*
church	igreja *ee-**gray**-JUH*
exhibition	exposição *esh-poo-zee-**souŋ***
gallery	galeria de arte *gUH-lae-**ree**-ya **dahr**-t*
modern art	arte moderna *ahr-t moo-**dehr**-nUH*
mosque	mesquita *mesh-**kee**-tUH*
museum	museu *moo-**sae**-oo*
painting	*(picture)* quadro *kwah-droo*; *(art)* pintura *peen-**too**-rUH*
park	parque *pahr-k*
ruins	ruínas *RRoo-ee-nUHsh*

sculpture	escultura *esh-kool-**too**-rUH*
statue	estátua *esh-**tah**-too-UH*
street map	mapa das ruas *mah-pUH dash RRoo-UHsh*
synagogue	sinagoga *see-nUH-**goh**-gUH*
tour guide	guia (turístico) *gee-UH (too-reesh-tee-koo)*
tourist	turista *too-**reesh**-tUH*
tourist information centre	posto de turismo *powsh-too dae too-**reesh**-moo*
town centre	centro da cidade *sain-troo dUH see-**dah**-d*

Expressing yourself

I'd like some information on …
queria informação sobre…
*ke-**ree**-ya een-foor-mUH-**soum** so-bre…*

can you tell me where the tourist information centre is?
pode dizer-me onde é o posto de turismo?
*poh-d dee-**zaer**-mae on-d eh oo **powsh**-too dae too-**reesh**-moo?*

do you have a street map of the town?
tem um mapa da cidade?
*taim oom **mah**-pUH dUH see-**dah**-d?*

what is there worth visiting?
o que há de interessante para visitar?
*oo ke ah dae een-te-re-**sUHn**-t pUH-rUH vee-zee-**tahr**?*

can you show me where it is on the map?
pode indicar-me onde fica no mapa?
*poh-d een-dee-**kahr**-mae on-d **fee**-kUH noo **mah**-pUH?*

how do you get there?
como é que lá chego?
*ko-moo eh ke lah **shae**-goo?*

is it free?
a entrada é grátis?
*UH ain-**trah**-dUH eh **grah**-teesh?*

when was it built?
quando foi construído/construída?
*kwUHn-doo **foy**-ee konsh-troo-**ee**-doo/konsh-troo-**ee**-dUH?*

Understanding

aberto	open
baixa	city centre
barroco/barroca	Baroque
circuito turístico	tourist trail
encerrado para obras	closed for renovation
entrada livre	admission free
fechado/fechada	closed
gótico/gótica	Gothic
guerra	war
invasão	invasion
manuelino/manuelina	Manueline
medieval	medieval
miradouro	viewpoint
mourisco/mourisca	Moorish
obras de restauro/renovação	restoration work
património da humanidade	world heritage site
românico/românica	Roman
visita guiada	guided tour
vista panorâmica	panoramic view
você está aqui	you are here *(on a map)*
zona histórica	old town
zona pedonal	pedestrian precinct

terá de perguntar quando lá chegar
you'll have to ask when you get there

a próxima visita guiada começa às duas (horas)
the next guided tour starts at 2 o'clock

MUSEUMS, EXHIBITIONS AND MONUMENTS

Expressing yourself

I've heard there's a very good ... exhibition on at the moment
ouvi dizer que neste momento há uma exposição muito boa sobre ...
*o-vee dee-zaer ke naesh-t moo-main-too ah oo-mUH esh-poo-zee-souŋ
mooy-too bo-UH so-bre ...*

how much is it to get in?
quanto custa a entrada?
kwUHn-too koosh-tUH UH ain-trah-dUH?

is this ticket valid for the exhibition as well?
este bilhete também é válido para a exposição?
aesh-t beel-yae-t tam-baim eh vah-lee-doo pUH-rUH UH esh-poo-zee-souŋ?

are there any discounts for students?
há desconto para estudantes?
ah desh-kon-too pUH-rUH esh-too-dUHn-tesh?

is it open on Sundays?
abre ao domingo?
ah-bre ow do-meen-goo?

I have a student card
tenho cartão de estudante
tain-yo kUHr-touŋ dae esh-too-dUHn-t

two concessions and one full price, please
dois bilhetes com desconto e um normal, se faz favor
doy-eesh beel-yae-tesh kom desh-kon-too ee oom nohr-mahl, s-fahsh fUH-vor

Understanding

audioguia	audioguide
bilheteira	ticket office
exposição permanente	permanent exhibition
exposição temporária	temporary exhibition
não tocar	please do not touch
proibido tirar fotografias	no photography
proibido usar flash	no flash photography
sentido da visita	this way
silêncio, por favor	silence, please

a entrada (no museu) custa…
admission to the museum costs …

tem cartão de estudante?
do you have a student card?

este bilhete também é válido para a exposição
this ticket also allows you access to the exhibition

GIVING YOUR IMPRESSIONS

Expressing yourself

it's beautiful
é lindo/linda
eh leen-doo/leen-dUH

it was beautiful
foi lindo/linda
foy-ee leen-doo/leen-dUH

it's fantastic
é fantástico/fantástica
eh fUHn-tahsh-tee-koo/fUHn-tahsh-tee-kUH

it was fantastic
foi fantástico/fantástica
foy-ee fUHn-tahsh-tee-koo/fUHn-tahsh-tee-kUH

I really enjoyed it
gostei muito
goosh-tay mooy-too

I didn't like it that much
não gostei muito
nouŋ goosh-tay mooy-too

it was a bit boring
foi um pouco aborrecido/aborrecida
foy-ee oom po-koo UH-boo-RRe-see-do/UH-boo-RRe-see-dUH

I'm not really a fan of modern art
não gosto muito de arte moderna
nouŋ gosh-too mooy-too dae ahr-t moo-dehr-nUH

it's expensive for what it is
demasiado caro para o que é
dae-mUH-zee-ah-doo kah-roo pUH-rUH oo ke eh

it's very touristy
demasiado turístico/turística
dae-mUH-zee-ah-doo too-reesh-tee-koo/too-reesh-tee-kUH

it was really crowded
havia demasiada gente
UH-vee-ya dae-mUH-zee-ah-dUH Jain-t

we didn't go in the end, the queue was too long
acabámos por não ir, a fila de espera era demasiado longa
UH-kUH-bah-moosh poor nouŋ eer, UH fee-lUH desh-peh-rUH eh-rUH dae-mUH-zee-ah-doo lon-gUH

we didn't have time to see everything
não tivemos tempo de ver tudo
noun tee-vae-moosh taim-poo dae vaer too-doo

Understanding

famoso/famosa	famous
pitoresco/pitoresca	picturesque
típico/típica	typical
tradicional	traditional

tem/têm de ver...
you really must go and see …

aconselho/recomendo que vá/vão a ...
I recommend going to …

a vista da cidade é lindíssima
the view of the city is beautiful

tornou-se demasiado turístico/turística
it's become a bit too touristy

a costa está completamente estragada
the coast has been completely ruined

Football is easily the most popular sport in Portugal. The teams with the biggest followings are Benfica, Sporting and Porto, with competition between the first two (both Lisbon teams) particularly fierce.

Hockey is also increasingly popular, as are the **Touradas** (bullfights), which are held from April to October. Portugal is famous the world over for its golf courses, as the sport can be enjoyed virtually all year round.

On an international level, the Portuguese have been particularly successful in athletics.

The basics

ball	bola *boh-lUH*
basketball	basquete(bol) *bahsh-keh-t(bohl)*
board game	jogo de tabuleiro *Jo-goo dae tUH-boo-lay-roo*
cards	cartas *kahr-tUHsh*
chess	xadrez *shUH-draysh*
cross-country skiing	esqui de fundo *esh-kee dae foon-doo*
cycling	ciclismo *see-kleesh-moo*
downhill skiing	esqui alpino *esh-kee ahl-pee-noo*
football	futebol *foo-t-bohl*
hiking path	percurso pedestre *per-koor-soo pe-dehsh-tre*
match	jogo *Jo-goo*
mountain biking	bicicleta de montanha *bee-see-kleh-tUH dae mon-tUHn-yUH*
pool *(game)*	bilhar *beel-yahr*
rugby	râguebi *RRUH-gee-bee*
sailing	(fazer) vela *(fUH-zaer) veh-lUH*
ski	esqui *esh-kee*
snowboarding	(fazer) snowboard *(fUH-zaer) snowboard*
sport	desporto *desh-por-too*
surfing	(fazer) surf *(fUH-zaer) surf*
swimming	nadar *nUH-dahr* natação *nUH-tUH-souŋ*

swimming pool	piscina *pee-see-nUH*
table football	matraquilhos *mUH-trUH-keel-yoosh*
tennis	ténis *teh-neesh*
to go hiking	fazer caminhada *fUH-zaer kUH-meen-yah-dUH*
to have a game of ...	jogar um jogo de ... *Joo-gahr oom Jo-goo dae ...*
to play	jogar *Joo-gahr*

Expressing yourself

I'd like to hire ... for an hour
queria alugar ... por uma hora
ke-ree-ya UH-loo-gahr ... poohr oo-mUH oh-rUH

are there ... lessons available?
é possível ter aulas de ...?
eh poo-see-vehl taer ow-lUHsh dae ...?

how much is it per person per hour?
quanto custa por hora por pessoa?
kwUHn-too koosh-tUH poohr oh-rUH poohr pe-so-UH?

I'm not very sporty
não sou muito desportista
noun so mooy-too desh-por-teesh-tUH

I've never done it before
nunca tentei
noon-kUH tain-tay

I've done it once or twice, a long time ago
tentei uma ou duas vezes, há muito tempo
tain-tay oo-mUH o doo-UHsh vae-zesh, ah mooy-too taim-poo

I'm exhausted!
estou exausto/exausta!
esh-to ee-zowsh-too/ee-zowsh-tUH!

I'd like to go and watch a football match
gostava de assistir a um jogo de futebol
goosh-tah-vUH dae UH-seesh-teer ah oom Jo-goo dae foo-t-bohl

we played...
jogámos...
Jo-gah-moosh...

Understanding

... para alugar ... for hire

já tem alguma experiência, ou é a primeira vez?
do you have any experience, or are you a complete beginner?

é preciso pagar um depósito de ...
there is a deposit of ...

o seguro é obrigatório e custa ...
insurance is compulsory and costs ...

HIKING

Expressing yourself

are there any hiking paths around here?
há algum percurso pedestre na zona?
ah ahl-goom per-koor-soo pe-desh-tre nUH zo-nUH?

can you recommend any good walks in the area?
pode recomendar-me algum passeio a pé nos arredores?
poh-d RRe-koo-main-dahr-mae al-goom pUH-say-oo UH peh noosh UH-RRe-doh-resh?

we're looking for a short walk somewhere round here
queríamos dar um pequeno passeio a pé por aqui perto
ke-ree-UH-moosh dahr oom pe-kae-noo pUH-say-oo UH peh poor UH-kee pehr-too

can I hire hiking boots?
gostava de alugar umas botas para caminhar
goosh-tah-vUH dae UH-loo-gahr oo-mUHsh boh-tUHsh pUH-rUH kUH-meen-yahr

how long does the hike take?
quanto tempo demora a caminhada?
kwUHn-too taim-poo dae-moh-rUH UH kUH-meen-yah-dUH?

is it very steep?
é muito a subir?
eh mooy-too UH soo-beer?

where's the start of the path?
onde é que começa o percurso?
on-d eh ke koo-meh-sUH oo per-koor-soo?

is the path waymarked?
o caminho está assinalado?
oo kUH-meen-yoo esh-tah UH-see-nUH-lah-doo?

is it a circular path?
o percurso começa e termina no mesmo sítio?
oo per-koor-soo koo-meh-sUH ee ter-mee-nUH noo maesh-moo see-tee-oo?

Understanding

duração média	average duration *(of walk)*
trilho de longo curso	long hike
trilho equestre	horse path

são cerca de três horas de marcha/caminhada incluindo pausas
it's about three hours' walk including rest stops

trazer um impermeável e calçado para caminhar
bring a waterproof jacket and walking shoes

OTHER SPORTS

Expressing yourself

where can we hire bikes?
onde podemos alugar bicicletas?
on-d poo-dae-moosh UH-loo-gahr bee-see-kleh-tUHsh?

are there any cycle paths?
há algum percurso para bicicletas na zona?
ah ahl-goom per-koor-soo pUH-rUH bee-see-kleh-tUHsh nUH zo-nUH?

does anyone have a football?
alguém tem uma bola de futebol?
ahl-gaim taim oo-mUH boh-lUH dae foo-t-bohl?

which team do you support?
qual é a sua equipa?
kwahl eh UH soo-UH e-kee-pUH?

I support ...
sou do ...
so doo ...

is there an open-air swimming pool?
há alguma piscina ao ar livre?
ah ahl-goo-mUH pee-see-nUH ow ahr lee-vre?

I've never been diving before
nunca fiz mergulho
noon-kUH feesh mer-gool-yoo

I'd like to take beginners' sailing lessons
gostava de ter algumas aulas de vela para principiantes
goosh-tah-vUH dae taer ahl-goo-mUHsh ahw-lUHsh dae veh-lUH pUH-rUH preen-see-pee-UHn-tesh

I run for half an hour every morning
todas as manhãs corro meia hora
to-dUHsh UHs mUHn-yUHsh ko-RRoo may-UH oh-rUH

what do I do if the kayak capsizes?
o que é que faço se o caiaque se virar?
oo ke eh ke fah-soo sae oo kaee-yah-ke sae vee-rahr?

Understanding

há um court/campo de ténis público perto da estação
there's a public tennis court not far from the station

o court/campo de ténis está ocupado
the tennis court's being used

é a primeira vez que monta a cavalo?
is this the first time you've been horse-riding?

sabe nadar?
can you swim?

joga basquete?
do you play basketball?

INDOOR GAMES

Expressing yourself

shall we have a game of cards?
vai um jogo de cartas?
vaee oom Jo-goo dae kahr-tUHsh?

does anyone know any good card games?
alguém conhece um bom jogo de cartas?
ahl-gaim kon-yeh-s oom bom Jo-goo dae kahr-tUHsh?

is anyone up for a game of Monopoly®?
alguém quer jogar monopólio?
ahl-gaim kehr Joo-gahr moo-noo-poh-lee-oo?

it's your turn
é a sua vez
eh UH soo-UH vaysh

Understanding

sabe jogar xadrez?
do you know how to play chess?

tem um baralho de cartas?
do you have a pack of cards?

Some informal expressions

estou estoirado/estoirada I'm totally knackered
deu-me uma lição he absolutely thrashed me

SHOPPING

Compared with other European countries, regional produce in Portugal is fairly cheap, particularly outside the main cities.

Shops are open from 9am to 1pm, then close for lunch and reopen from 3pm to 7pm (though times may vary according to the region). Small shops tend to close on Saturday afternoons and Sundays. Portuguese markets are a real occasion, full of life and colour. Most towns have their own markets; they start very early in the morning and haggling is perfectly acceptable.

There are sales at the beginning of January and the end of August. Large supermarkets are usually located on the outskirts of town. Popular chain stores in Portugal include **Modelo**, **Continente**, **Pingo Doce**, **Feira Nova** and **Jumbo**.

Some informal expressions

custa os olhos da cara it costs an arm and a leg
é um roubo! that's a rip-off!
é uma pechincha! it's a bargain!
não tenho um tostão I'm skint
ver montras window shopping

The basics

bakery	padaria *pah-dUH-**ree**-ya*
butcher's	talho *tahl-yo*
cash desk	caixa *kaee-shUH*
cheap	barato/barata *bUH-**rah**-too/bUH-**rah**-tUH*
checkout	caixa *kaee-shUH*
clothes	roupa *RRo-pUH*, vestuário *vesh-too-**ah**-ryoo*
department store	grande loja *grUHn-d loh-JUH*, armazém *ahr-mUH-**zaim***

expensive	caro/cara *kah-roo/kah-rUH*
gram	grama *grUH-mUH*
greengrocer's	loja de verduras *loh-JUH dae ver-doo-rUHsh*, mercearia *mer-sae-UH-ree-ya*
hypermarket	hipermercado *ee-pehr-mer-kah-doo*
kilo	quilo *kee-loo*
present	prenda *prain-dUH*, presente *pre-zain-t*
price	preço *prae-soo*
receipt	recibo *RRe-see-boo*, talão *tUH-louŋ*
refund	reembolso *RRe-aim-bol-soo*
sales	saldos *sahl-doosh*
sales assistant	vendedor/vendedora *vain-dae-dor/vain-dae-do-rUH*
shop	loja *loh-JUH*
shopping centre	centro comercial *sain-troo koo-mer-see-ahl*
souvenir	lembrança *laim-brUHn-sUH*
supermarket	supermercado *soo-pehr-mer-kah-doo*
to buy	comprar *kom-prahr*
to cost	custar *koosh-tahr*
to go shopping	ir às compras *eer ahsh kom-prUHsh*
to pay	pagar *pUH-gahr*
to refund	reembolsar *RRe-aim-bol-sahr*
to sell	vender *vain-daer*
to shop	fazer compras *fUH-zaer kom-prUHsh*

SHOPPING

Expressing yourself

is there a supermarket near here?
há algum supermercado aqui perto?
ah ahl-goom soo-pehr-mer-kah-doo UH-kee pehr-too?

where can I buy cigarettes?
onde posso comprar cigarros?
on-d poh-soo kom-prahr see-gah-RRoosh?

I'd like …
queria …
ke-ree-ya …

I'm looking for …
procuro …
proh-koo-roo …

do you sell …?
tem/vende …?
taim/vain-d …?

83

do you know where I might find some …?
sabe onde posso encontrar …?
sah-b on-d poh-soo ain-kon-trahr …?

can you order it for me?
pode encomendar um/uma para mim?
poh-d ain-koo-main-dahr oom/oo-mUH pUH-rUH meem?

how much is this?
quanto custa (isto)?
kwUHn-too koosh-tUH (eesh-too)?

I'll take it
fico com ele/ela
fee-koo kom ae-l/eh-lUH

I haven't got much money
não tenho muito dinheiro
noun tain-yo mooy-too deen-yay-roo

I haven't got enough money
não tenho dinheiro que chegue
noun tain-yo deen-yay-roo ke shae-g

that's everything, thanks
é tudo, obrigado/obrigada
eh too-doo, o-bree-gah-doo/o-bree-gah-dUH

can I have a (plastic) bag?
podia dar-me uma saca (de plástico)?
poo-dee-ya dahr-mae oo-mUH sah-kUH (dae plahsh-tee-koo)?

I think you've made a mistake with my change
creio que se enganou no troco
kray-oo ke se ain-gUH-noo noo tro-koo

Understanding

aberto das … às …
open from … to …

fechado aos domingos/entre as 13h e as 15h
closed Sundays/1pm to 3pm

horário de atendimento/funcionamento
opening hours

promoção/oferta especial
special offer

saldos
sales

mais alguma coisa?
will there be anything else?

quer um saco?
would you like a bag?

PAYING

SHOPPING

Expressing yourself

where do I pay?
onde pago?
on-d pah-goo?

how much do I owe you?
quanto devo?
kwUHn-too dae-voo?

could you write it down for me, please?
importa-se de escrever quanto é?
eem-pohr-tUH-sae desh-kre-vaer kwUHn-too eh?

can I pay by credit card?
posso pagar com cartão de crédito?
poh-soo pUH-gahr kom kUHr-touŋ dae kreh-dee-too?

I'll pay in cash
vou pagar em dinheiro
vo pUH-gahr aim deen-yay-roo

can I have a receipt?
pode dar-me um recibo?
poh-d dahr-mae oom RRe-see-boo?

I'm sorry, I haven't got any change
desculpe, mas não tenho dinheiro trocado
desh-kool-p, mUHsh nouŋ tain-yo deen-yay-roo troo-kah-doo

Understanding

pagar na caixa
pay at the cash desk

assine aqui, se faz favor
sign here, please

como deseja/vai pagar?
how would you like to pay?

tem mais pequeno?
do you have anything smaller?

tem um documento de identificação?
have you got any ID?

FOOD

Expressing yourself

where can I buy food around here?
onde posso comprar comida aqui perto?
on-d poh-soo kom-prahr koo-mee-dUH UH-kee pehr-too?

is there a market?
há algum mercado?
ah ahl-goom mer-kah-doo?

is there a bakery around here?
há alguma padaria perto?
ah ahl-goo-mUH pah-dUH-ree-ya pehr-too?

I'm looking for the cereal aisle
procuro a secção dos cereais
proh-koo-roo UH sehk-souη doosh se-re-aeesh

I'd like five slices of ham
queria cinco fatias de fiambre
ke-ree-ya seen-koo fUH-tee-UHsh dae fee-UHm-bre

I'd like some goat's cheese
queria queijo de cabra
ke-ree-ya kay-Joo dae kah-brUH

it's for four people
é para quatro pessoas
eh pUH-rUH kwah-troo pe-so-UHsh

about 300 grams
cerca de trezentas gramas
saer-kUH dae trae-zain-tUHsh grUH-mUHsh

a kilo of apples, please
um quilo de maçãs, se faz favor
oom kee-loo dae mUH-sUHηsh, s-fahsh fUH-vor

a bit less/more
um pouco menos/mais
oom po-koo mae-noosh/my-sh

can I taste it?
posso provar?
poh-soo proo-vahr?

does it travel well?
viaja bem?
vee-ah-jUH baim?

Understanding

caseiro/caseira	homemade
charcutaria	delicatessen
consumir de preferência antes de...	best before ...
especialidades regionais	local specialities

orgânico/orgânica organic

há um mercado todas as manhãs até à uma
there's a market every morning until 1pm

há uma loja mesmo à esquina que está aberta até tarde
there's a grocer's just on the corner that's open late

CLOTHES

Expressing yourself

I'm looking for the menswear section
procuro a secção para homens
proh-koo-roo UH sehk-soun pUH-rUH oh-mainsh

no thanks, I'm just looking
não obrigado/obrigada, estou só a ver
noun o-bree-gah-doo/o-bree-gah-dUH, esh-to soh UH vaer

can I try it on?
posso experimentar?
poh-soo esh-pe-ree-main-tahr?

I'd like to try the one in the window
queria experimentar o/a que está na montra
ke-ree-ya esh-pe-ree-main-tahr oo/UH ke esh-tah nUH mon-trUH

I take a size 39 *(in shoes)*
calço 39
kahl-soo treen-tUH ee noh-v

where are the changing rooms?
onde são as cabines de provas?
on-d soun UHsh kah-bee-nesh dae proh-vUHsh?

it doesn't fit
não me serve
noun mae sehr-v

it's too big/small
é demasiado grande/pequeno/pequena
eh dae-mah-zee-ah-doo grUHn-d/pee-kae-noo/pee-kae-nUH

do you have them in red?
tem em vermelho?
taim aim ver-mael-yoo?

do you have it in another colour?
tem outras cores?
taim o-trUHsh ko-resh?

do you have it in a smaller/bigger size?
tem em tamanho/um número maior/mais pequeno?
taim aim tUH-mahn-yo/oom noo-mae-roo mUH-ee-ohr/my-sh pe-kae-noo?

yes, that's fine, I'll take them
sim, estes/estas estão bem, levo-os/levo-as
seem, aesh-tesh/ehsh-tUHsh esh-toun baim, leh-voo-oosh/leh-voo-UHsh

no, I don't like it
não gosto
noun gohsh-too

I'll think about it
vou pensar
vo pain-sahr

I'd like to return this, it doesn't fit
queria devolver isto, não me serve
ke-ree-ya de-vohl-vaer eesh-too, noun mae sehr-v

this... has a hole in it, can I get a refund?
este/esta... tem um buraco, posso ser reembolsado/reembolsada?
aesh-t/ehsh-tUH... taim oom boo-rah-koo, poh-soo saer RRe-aim-bol-sah-doo/RRe-aim-bol-sah-dUH?

Understanding

aberto aos domingos	open Sundays
artigos em saldo não são trocados	sale items cannot be returned
cabines de provas	changing rooms
roupa de criança	children's clothes
roupa de homem	menswear
roupa de senhora	ladieswear

posso ajudar?
can I help you?

já só temos em azul e preto
we only have it in blue or black

já não temos nesse número/tamanho
we don't have any left in that size

fica-lhe bem
it suits you

cai-lhe/assenta-lhe bem
it's a good fit

se não lhe servir pode devolver
you can bring it back if it doesn't fit

SOUVENIRS AND PRESENTS

Expressing yourself

I'm looking for a present to take home
procuro uma prenda/uma lembrança para levar
*proh-koo-roo oo-mUH prain-dUH/oo-mUH laim-brUHn-sUH pUH-rUH
lae-vahr*

I'd like something that's easy to transport
queria alguma coisa fácil de transportar
ke-ree-ya ahl-goo-mUH koy-zUH fah-seel dae trUHnsh-poor-tahr

it's for a little girl of four
é para uma menina de quatro anos
eh pUH-rUH oo-mUH mae-nee-nUH dae kwah-troo UH-noosh

could you gift-wrap it for me?
pode embrulhar? é para oferecer
poh-d aim-brool-yahr? eh pUH-rUH oh-fe-re-saer

Understanding

de madeira/prata/ ouro/lã	made of wood/silver/gold/wool
feito à mão	handmade
produto artesanal	traditionally made product

quanto quer gastar?
how much do you want to spend?

é para oferecer?
is it for a present?

é típico/típica da região
it's typical of the region

PHOTOS

The basics

black and white	preto e branco *prae-too ee brUHn-koo*
camera	máquina fotográfica *mah-kee-nUH foo-too-grah-fee-kUH*, câmara (fotográfica) *kUH-mUH-rUH (foo-too-grah-fee-kUH)*
colour	a cores *UH ko-resh*
copy	cópia *koh-pee-ya*
digital camera	câmara digital *kUH-mUH-rUH dee-Jee-tahl*, máquina digital *mah-kee-nUH dee-Jee-tahl*
disposable camera	máquina descartável *mah-kee-nUH desh-kUHr-tah-vehl*, câmara descartável *kUH-mUH-rUH desh-kUHr-tah-vehl*
exposure	exposição *esh-poo-zee-souŋ*
film	rolo (fotográfico) *RRo-loo (foo-too-grah-fee-koo)*
flash	flash *flah-sh*
glossy	brilhante *breel-yUHn-t*, com brilho *kom breel-yo*
matt	mate *mah-t*, sem brilho *saim breel-yo*
memory card	cartão para máquina digital *kUHr-touŋ pUH-rUH mah-kee-nUH dee-Jee-tahl*
negative	negativo *ne-gUH-tee-voo*
passport photo	fotografia tipo passe *foo-too-grUH-fee-UH tee-poo pah-s*
photo booth	Fotomatom® *foh-toh-mah-tom*
reprint	cópia *koh-pee-ya*
slide	slide *slide* diapositivo *dee-UH-poo-zee-tee-voo*
to get photos developed	mandar revelar fotografias *mUHn-dahr RRe-ve-lahr foo-too-grUH-fee-UHsh*
to take a photo/ photos	tirar uma fotografia/fotografias *tee-rahr oo-mUH foo-too-grUH-feeUH/foo-too-grUH-fee-UHsh*

PHOTOS

Expressing yourself

could you take a photo of us, please?
importa-se de nos tirar uma fotografia, se faz favor?
eem-pohr-tUH-sae dae noosh tee-rahr oo-mUH foo-too-grUH-fee-UH, s-fahsh fUH-vor?

you just have to press here/this button
basta carregar aqui/neste botão
bahsh-tUH kUH-RRe-gahr UH-kee/naesh-t boo-touŋ

I'd like a 200 ASA colour film
queria um rolo a cores de duzentos ASA
ke-ree-ya oom RRo-loo UH ko-resh dae doo-zain-toosh ah-zUH

do you have black and white films?
tem rolos para fotografias a preto e branco?
taim RRo-loosh pUH-rUH foo-too-grUH-fee-UHsh UH prae-too ee brUHn-koo?

how much is it to develop a film of 36 photos?
quanto custa revelar um rolo de trinta e seis fotografias?
kwUHn-too koosh-tUH RRe-ve-lahr oom RRo-loo dae treen-tUH ee saysh foo-too-grUH-fee-UHsh?

I'd like to have this film developed
queria revelar este rolo
ke-ree-ya RRe-ve-lahr aesh-t RRo-loo

I'd like extra copies of some of the photos
queria fazer cópias de algumas das fotografias
ke-ree-ya fUH-zaer koh-pee-UHsh dal-goo-mUHsh dUHsh foo-too-grUH-fee-UHsh

three copies of this one and two of this one
três cópias desta e duas desta
traysh koh-pee-UHsh dehsh-tUH ee doo-UHsh dehsh-tUH

can I print my digital photos here?
posso imprimir as minhas fotografias (digitais) aqui?
poh-soo eem-pre-meer UHsh meen-yUHsh foo-too-grUH-fee-UHsh (dee-Jee-tah-eesh) UH-kee?

do you sell memory cards?
vende cartões para máquinas digitais?
vain-d kUHr-toiŋsh pUH-rUH mah-kee-nUHsh dee-Jee-tah-eesh?

can you put these photos on a CD for me?
pode passar-me estas fotografias para um CD?
poh-d pUH-sahr-mae ehsh-tUHsh foo-too-grUH-fee-UHsh pUH-rUH oom say-day?

I've come to pick up my photos
venho buscar as minhas fotografias
vain-yo boosh-kahr UHsh meen-yUHsh foo-too-grUH-fee-UHsh

I've got a problem with my camera
tenho um problema com a minha máquina (fotográfica)
tain-yo oom proo-blae-mUH kom UH meen-yUH mah-kee-nUH (foo-too-grah-fee-kUH)

I don't know what it is	**the flash doesn't work**
não sei o que é	o flash não funciona
nouŋ say oo ke eh	*oo flah-sh nouŋ foon-see-o-nUH*

Understanding

formato normal	standard format
fotografias em CD	photos on CD
revelação numa hora	photos developed in one hour
serviço expresso	express service

talvez a pilha esteja gasta
maybe the battery's dead

temos uma máquina para imprimir fotografias digitais
we have a machine for printing digital photos

(qual é) o nome, por favor?	**para quando (as quer)?**
what's the name, please?	when do you want them for?

podem estar prontas numa hora
we can develop them in an hour

pode levantar as suas fotografias na quinta-feira a partir do meio-dia
your photos will be ready on Thursday from noon

BANKS

Banks are open from 8.30am to 3pm, Monday to Friday. Branches found in supermarkets tend to have more flexible opening hours. There are plenty of cash machines available, from which you can withdraw money using most bank cards – look out for the blue **MB** logo.

The basics

bank	banco *bUHn-koo*
bank account	conta bancária *kon-tUH bUHn-kah-ree-ya*
banknote	nota *noh-tUH*
bureau de change	casa de câmbio *kah-ZUH dae kUHm-bee-yo*
cashpoint	caixa automático *kaee-shUH ow-too-mah-tee-koo,* Multibanco *mool-tee-bUHn-koo*
change	câmbio *kUHm-bee-yo*
cheque	cheque *sheh-k*
coin	moeda *moo-eh-dUH*
commission	comissão *koo-mee-souŋ*
credit card	cartão de crédito *kUHr-touŋ dae kreh-dee-too*
PIN (number)	código pessoal *koh-dee-goo pe-soo-ahl*
transfer	transferência *trUHns-fe-rain-see-ya*
Travellers Cheques®	cheques de viagem *sheh-kesh dae vee-ah-jaim*
withdrawal	levantamento *le-vUHn-tUH-main-too*
to change	trocar *troo-kahr*
to withdraw	levantar (dinheiro) *le-vUHn-tahr (deen-yay-roo)*

Expressing yourself

where can I get some money changed?
onde posso trocar dinheiro?
on-d poh-soo troo-kahr deen-yay-roo?

are banks open on Saturdays?
os bancos abrem ao sábado?
oosh bUHn-koosh ah-braim UH-oo sah-bUH-doo?

I'm looking for a cashpoint
procuro um Multibanco
proh-koo-roo oom mool-tee-bUHn-koo

I'd like to change £100
queria trocar cem libras
ke-ree-ya troo-kahr saim lee-brUHsh

what commission do you charge?
quanto é a comissão?
kwUHn-too eh UH koo-mee-souη?

I'd like to transfer some money
queria transferir dinheiro
ke-ree-ya trUHns-fe-reer deen-yay-roo

I'd like to report the loss of my credit card
queria participar a perda do meu cartão de crédito
ke-ree-ya pUHr-tee-see-pahr UH paer-dUH doo mae-oo kUHr-touη dae kreh-dee-too

the cashpoint has swallowed my card
o Multibanco ficou com o meu cartão
oo mool-tee-bUHn-koo fee-ko kom oo mae-oo kUHr-touη

Understanding

insira o seu cartão
please insert your card

marque o seu código pessoal
please enter your PIN number

seleccione o montante
please select amount for withdrawal

levantamento sem recibo
withdrawal without receipt

levantamento com recibo
withdrawal with receipt

fora de serviço
out of service

POST OFFICES

Post offices can be identified by a blue **CTT** sign, and a logo depicting a messenger on a white horse against a red background. Blue letter boxes are for **correio azul** (fast service), while red ones are for regular post. Inside post offices (and sometimes on the wall outside) you will find separate post boxes for national and international mail. An express mail service (**EMS**) is available, as well as a recorded delivery service.

You can buy stamps in post offices, some kiosks and shops displaying the red and white logo. Stamp vending machines can be found in some airports and railway stations.

Post offices are generally open from 8.30am to 6.30pm, Monday to Friday (and Saturday at airports).

The basics

address	endereço *ain-de-rae-soo*
airmail	correio aéreo *koo-RRay-oo UH-eh-ree-oo*
envelope	envelope *ain-ve-loh-p*
letter	carta *kahr-tUH*
mail	correio *koo-RRay-oo*
parcel	encomenda *ain-koo-main-dUH,* pacote *pUH-koh-t*
post	correio *koo-RRay-oo*
postbox	caixa do correio *kah-ee-shUH doo koo-RRay-oo,* marco do correio *mahr-koo doo koo-RRay-oo*
postcard	postal *poosh-tahl*
postcode	código postal *koh-dee-goo poosh-tahl*
post office	(estação de) correios *(esh-tUH-souŋ dae) koo-RRay-oosh*
stamp	selo *sae-loo*
to post	pôr no correio *pour noo koo-RRay-oo*
to send	enviar *ain-vee-ahr*

Expressing yourself

is there a post office around here?
há alguma estação de correios perto?
ah ahl-goo-mUH esh-tUH-souη dae koo-RRay-oosh pehr-too?

is there a postbox near here?
há algum marco do correio perto?
ah ahl-goom mahr-koo doo koo-RRay-oo pehr-to?

is the post office open on Saturdays?
os correios abrem ao sábado?
oosh koo-RRay-oosh ah-braim UH-oo sah-bUH-doo?

what time does the post office close?
a que horas fecham os correios?
UH ke oh-rUHsh fae-shUHm oosh koo-RRay-oosh?

do you sell stamps?
vende selos?
vain-d sae-loosh?

I'd like … stamps for the UK, please
queria … selos para o Reino Unido, se faz favor
ke-ree-ya … sae-loosh pUH-rUH oo RRay-noo oo-nee-doo, s-fahsh fUH-vor

how much is a stamp for Scotland?
quanto custa um selo para a Escócia?
kwUHn-too koosh-tUH oom sae-loo pUH-rUH UH esh-koh-see-ya?

how much would it be to send this/this package?
quanto custa enviar isto/este pacote?
kwUHn-too koosh-tUH ain-vee-ahr eesh-too/aesh-t pUH-koh-t?

how long will it take to arrive?
quanto tempo demora a chegar?
kwUHn-too taim-poo dae-moh-rUH UH shae-gahr?

where can I buy envelopes?
onde posso comprar envelopes?
on-d poh-soo kom-prahr ain-ve-loh-pesh?

is there any post for me?
há correio para mim?
ah koo-RRay-oo pUH-rUH meem?

Understanding

carta registada	recorded letter
carteiro	postman
destinatário	addressee
frágil	handle with care/fragile
franquia/tarifa postal	postage
primeira recolha	first collection
remetente	sender
última recolha	last collection

(para comprar) selos, é no guiché ao lado
for stamps go to the next counter

quer enviar por correio normal ou por correio azul?
do you want to sent it by normal post or fast service?

leva/demora entre três a cinco dias
it'll take between three and five days

fica em 10 euros
it will cost you 10 euros

Understanding addresses

A/C	= ao cuidado de	care of
Av.	= avenida	avenue
Dt.°	= direito	right
Esq.°	= esquerdo	left
Pr.	= praça	square
R.	= rua	street
R/c	= rés-do-chão	basement

House numbers are written after the name of the street.

INTERNET CAFÉS AND E-MAIL

Internet cafés in Portugal are only common in the bigger cities and towns but most post offices now have terminals for NetFast, an Internet facility payable with a special card. Municipal libraries and municipality-run **ciber-espaços** offer offer free Internet access.

The "at" sign is called an **arroba** (*UH-RRo-bUH*), a dot is a **ponto** (*pon-too*) and a dash is a **traço** (*trah-soo*). **Todo junto** (*too-doo Joon-too*) means that a part of the address is all one word. So, for example, the address mariasilva@sapo.pt would be given as "**maria silva (tudo junto) arroba sapo ponto pt**" (*mUH-ree-a-seel-vUH too-doo Joon-too UH-RRo-bUH sah-poo pon-too pay-tay*).

The basics

at sign	arroba *UH-RRo-bUH*
e-mail	correio electrónico *koo-RRay-oo ee-leh-troh-nee-koo*, e-mail *e-mail*
e-mail address	endereço de correio electrónico/de e-mail *ain-de-rae-soo dae koo-RRay-oo ee-leh-troh-nee-koo/de-mail*
file ·	ficheiro *fee-shay-roo*
Internet café	ciber-café *see-behr kUH-feh*, Internet café *een-tehr-neh-t kUH-feh*
key	tecla *teh-klUH*
keyboard	teclado *teh-klah-doo*
new	novo *no-voo*
to close	fechar *fae-shahr*
to copy	copiar *koo-pee-ahr*
to cut	cortar *koor-tahr*
to delete	apagar *UH-pUH-gahr*
to download	descarregar *desh-kUH-RRe-gahr*, fazer o download de *fUH-zaehr oo download dae*

to e-mail somebody	enviar um e-mail a alguém *ain-vee-**ahr** oom e-mail UH ahl-**gaim***
to exit	sair *sUH-eer*
to open	abrir *UH-**breer***
to paste	colar *koo-**lahr***
to print	imprimir *eem-pree-**meer***
to receive	receber *RRe-se-**bae-r***
to save	guardar *gwUHr-**dahr***
to search	pesquisar *pesh-kee-**zahr***, buscar *boosh-**kahr***
to send an e-mail	enviar um e-mail *ain-vee-**ahr** oom e-**mail***

Expressing yourself

is there an Internet café near here?
há algum café com Internet aqui perto?
*ah ahl-**goom** KUH-**feh** kom een-tehr-**neh**-t UH-**kee** pehr-too?*

do you have an e-mail address?
tem endereço de e-mail?
*taim ain-dae-**rae**-soo de-**mail**?*

my e-mail address is alan_two@o-net.com
o meu endereço de e-mail é alan_two@o-net.com
*oo **mae**-oo ain-dae-**rae**-soo dee-**mail** eh ah-lUHn **trah**-soo two UH-**RRo**-bUH oh ee-**fain** neh-t **pon**-too kom*

how do I get online?
como é que ligo à Internet?
*ko-moo eh ke **lee**-goo ah een-tehr-**neh**-t?*

I'd just like to check my e-mails
só queria verificar o meu e-mail
*soh ke-**ree**-ya vae-ree-fee-**kahr** oo **mae**-oo e-**mail***

would you mind helping me, I'm not sure what to do
pode ajudar-me, não sei exactamente o que preciso de fazer
*poh-d UH-Joo-**dahr**-mae, nouɲ say ee-zah-tUH-**main**-t oo ke prae-**see**-zoo dae fUH-**zaer***

I can't find the at sign on this keyboard
não encontro a arroba neste teclado
*nouɲ ain-**kon**-troo UH UH-**RRo**-bUH **naesh**-t teh-**klah**-doo*

it's not working
não funciona
noun foon-see-o-nUH

there's something wrong with the computer, it's frozen
passa-se alguma coisa com o computador, o ecrã congelou
pUH-sUH-sae ahl-goo-mUH koy-zUH kom oo kom-poo-tUH-dor, oo eh-krUHη kon-Jae-lo

how much will it be for half an hour?
quanto custa meia hora?
kwUHn-too koosh-tUH may-UH oh-rUH?

when do I pay?
quando é que pago?
kwUHn-doo eh ke pah-goo?

Understanding

caixa de chegada   inbox
caixa de envio   outbox

tem de espera uns 20 minutos
you'll have to wait for 20 minutes or so

se tiver problemas avise
if you have any problems just let me know

pergunte se não souber o que fazer
just ask if you're not sure what to do

basta introduzir esta password/palavra-chave para entrar
just enter this password to log on

TELEPHONE

Telephone numbers are usually given one digit at a time in Portuguese, as in English, although there are no hard and fast rules. Zero is pronounced "*zeh-roo*". If a digit is repeated, it is pronounced as two separate digits (for example "44" is pronounced "*kwah-troo kwah-troo*").

British-style red telephone boxes can be found in Portugal, although the more modern ones tend to be the booth type and are beige. The Portugal Telecom phonecard is mainly used in Lisbon and Porto; Credifone cards are more common in the rest of the country. You can buy phonecards in Portugal Telecom shops, post offices, some kiosks and tobacconists. Some payphones also accept credit cards.

To call Portugal from abroad, dial 00 + 351 + the 9-digit number; to call the UK from Portugal, dial 00 + 44, then drop the first 0 of the UK area code. To call the US, dial 00 + 1 followed by the area code and phone number.

The basics

answering machine	atendedor de chamadas *UH-tain-dae-dor dae shUH-mah-dUHsh*
call	chamada *shUH-mah-dUH*, telefonema *te-le-foo-nae-mUH*
directory enquiries	informações *een-foor-mUH-soiŋsh*
hello	*(when calling)* está *esh-tah; (when answering)* estou *esh-to*
international call	chamada internacional *shUH-mah-dUH een-ter-nUH-see-o-nahl*
local call	chamada local *shUH-mah-dUH loo-kahl*
message	mensagem *main-sah-Jaim*
mobile	telemóvel *teh-leh-moh-vehl*
national call	chamada nacional *shUH-mah-dUH nUH-see-oo-nahl*
phone	telefone *te-le-foh-n*

phone book	lista telefónica *leesh-tUH te-le-foh-nee-kUH*
phone box	cabine telefónica *kah-bee-n te-le-foh-nee-kUH*
phone call	chamada *shUH-mah-dUH*, telefonema *te-le-foo-nae-mUH*
phone number	número de telefone *noo-mae-roo dae te-le-foh-n*
phonecard	cartão telefónico *kUHr-touŋ te-le-foh-nee-koo*
ringtone	sinal *see-nahl*
telephone	telefone *te-le-foh-n*
top-up card	cartão de telemóvel *kUHr-touŋ dae teh-leh-moh-vehl*
Yellow Pages®	Páginas Amarelas® *pah-Jee-nUHsh UH-mUH-reh-lUHsh*
to call somebody	telefonar a alguém *te-le-foo-nahr UH ahl-gaim*

Expressing yourself

where can I buy a phonecard?
onde posso comprar um cartão telefónico?
on-d poh-soo kom-prahr oom kUHr-touŋ te-le-foh-nee-koo?

a ...-euro top-up card, please
queria um cartão de ... euros para o meu telemóvel, se faz favor
ke-ree-ya oom kUHr-touŋ dae ... aeoo-roosh pUH-rUH oo mae-oo teh-leh-moh-vehl, s-fahsh fUH-vor

I'd like to make a reverse-charge call
queria fazer uma chamada a cobrar no destino
ke-ree-ya fUH-zer oo-mUH shUH-mah-dUH UH koo-brahr noo desh-tee-noo

is there a phone box near here, please?
sabe se há alguma cabine telefónica aqui perto?
sah-b sae ah ahl-goo-mUH kah-bee-n te-le-foh-nee-kUH UH-kee pehr-too?

can I plug my phone in here to recharge it?
posso ligar o meu telemóvel aqui para recarregar?
poh-soo lee-gahr oo mae-oo teh-leh-moh-vehl UH-kee pUH-rUH RRe-kUH-RRe-gahr?

do you have a mobile number?
tem (um número de) telemóvel?
taim (oom noo-mae-roo dae) teh-leh-moh-vehl?

where can I contact you?
como o posso contactar?
ko-moo oo poh-soo kon-tUH-tahr?

did you get my message?
recebeu a minha mensagem?
RRe-se-bae-oo UH meen-ya main-sah-Jaim?

Understanding

o número que marcou não se encontra atribuído
the number you have dialled has not been recognized

carregue na tecla de cardinal
please press the hash key

MAKING A CALL

Expressing yourself

hello, this is David Brown (speaking)
está? aqui fala David Brown
esh-tah? UH-kee fah-lUH David Brown

hello? could I speak to..., please?
está? queria falar com..., se faz favor
esh-tah, ke-ree-ya fUH-lahr kom ..., s-fahsh fUH-vor

hello, is that Isabel?
está? é a Isabel?
esh-tah? eh UH ee-zUH-behl?

do you speak English?
fala inglês?
fah-lUH een-glaysh?

could you speak more slowly, please?
importa-se de falar mais devagar, se faz favor?
eem-pohr-tUH-sae dae fUH-lahr my-sh dae-vUH-gahr, s-fahsh fUH-vor?

I can't hear you, could you speak up, please?
não o/a consigo ouvir, importa-se de falar mais alto?
noun̠ oo/UH kon-see-go o-veer, eem-pohr-tUH-sae dae fUH-lahr my-sh ahl-too?

could you tell him/her I called?
podia dizer-lhe que telefonei?
*poo-**dee**-ya dee-**zaer**-lyae ke te-le-foo-**nay**?*

could you ask him/her to call me back?
importa-se de lhe dizer para me telefonar?
*eem-**pohr**-tUH-sae dae lyae dee-**zaer** p**UH**-rUH mae te-le-foo-**nahr**?*

I'll call back later
eu volto a telefonar
*ae-oo **vohl**-too UH te-le-foo-**nahr***

my name is … and my number is …
o meu nome é … e o meu número é …
*oo **mae**-oo **no**-m eh … ee oo **mae**-oo **noo**-mae-roo eh …*

do you know when he/she might be available?
quando é que eu posso falar com ele/ela?
*kw**UH**n-doo eh ke ae-oo **poh**-soo f**UH**-**lahr** kom ae-l/eh-l**UH**?*

thank you, goodbye
obrigado/obrigada, adeus
*oo-bree-**gah**-doo/oo-bree-**gah**-dUH, UH-**dae**-oosh*

Understanding

quem fala?
who's calling?

quer deixar recado?
do you want to leave a message?

dir-lhe-ei para lhe telefonar
I'll ask him/her to call you back

aguarde um momento
hold on

vou passar-lho/passar-lha
I'll just hand you over to him/her

enganou-se no número
you've got the wrong number

ele/ela não está
he's/she's not here at the moment

dir-lhe-ei que telefonou
I'll tell him/her you called

PROBLEMS

Expressing yourself

I don't know the code
não sei qual é o indicativo
nouη say kwahl eh oo een-dee-kUH-tee-voo

it's engaged
dá sinal de ocupado
dah see-nahl doh-koo-pah-doo

there's no reply
ninguém atende
neen-gaim UH-tain-d

I couldn't get through
não consegui ligar
nouη kon-sae-gee lee-gahr

I can't get a signal
não tenho rede
nouη tain-yoo RRae-d

I don't have much credit left on my phone
estou quase sem crédito no meu telemóvel
esh-to kwah-z saim kreh-dee-too noo mae-oo teh-leh-moh-vehl

we're about to get cut off
vamos ficar sem linha
vUH-moosh fee-kahr saim leen-yah

the reception's really bad here
a recepção é muito má aqui
UH RRe-saep-souη eh mooy-too mah UH-kee

Understanding

estou a ouvi-lo/ouvi-la muito mal
I can hardly hear you

a ligação é péssima
it's a bad line

Some informal expressions

fazer uma chamada to make a call
desligar o telefone na cara de alguém to hang up on somebody

TELEPHONE

HEALTH

If you are an EU national, pick up an E111 form from the Post Office before you go. This ensures that the cost of any medical treatment you may need in Portugal will be refunded to you when you return home, on production of a receipt. In order to have the cost of your treatment refunded, you must see a GP before visiting a specialist.

Pharmacies are open from 9am to 1pm and from 3pm to 7pm. A sign on the door gives the address of the nearest duty pharmacist. Many medicines which require a prescription in other countries are available over the counter in Portugal. Only pharmacies are licensed to sell medicines.

The number for the emergency services is 112.

The basics

allergy	alergia *UH-ler-Jee-UH*
ambulance	ambulância *UHm-boo-lUHn-see-ya*
aspirin	aspirina *UHsh-pee-ree-nUH*
blister	bolha (de água) *bol-yUH (dah-gwUH)*
blood	sangue *sUHn-g*
broken	partido/partida *pUHr-tee-doo/pUHr-tee-dUH*
burn	queimadura *kay-mUH-doo-rUH*
casualty (department)	urgências *oor-Jain-see-yUHsh*
chemist's	farmácia *fUHr-mah-see-ya*
cold	constipação *konsh-tee-pUH-souŋ*
condom	preservativo *pre-zaer-vUH-tee-voo*
constipation	prisão de ventre *pree-zouŋ dae vain-tre*
cough	tosse *toh-s*
dentist	dentista *dain-teesh-tUH*
diarrhoea	diarreia *dee-UH-RRay-UH*
doctor	médico *meh-dee-koo*
flu	gripe *gree-p*
food poisoning	intoxicação alimentar *een-tok-see-kUH-souŋ UH-lee-main-tahr*

GP	médico (de família) *meh-dee-koo (dae fUH-mee-lee-ya)*, clínico geral *klee-nee-koo Jae-rahl*
gynaecologist	ginecologista *Jee-nae-koo-loo-Jeesh-tUH*
hospital	hospital *ohsh-pee-tahl*
infection	infecção *een-fehk-souŋ*
medicine	medicamento *me-dee-kUH-main-too*, remédio *RRe-meh-dee-oo*
painkiller	analgésico *UH-nahl-Jeh-zee-koo*
period	período *pe-ree-oo-doo*, menstruação *mainsh-troo-UH-souŋ*
plaster	penso (rápido) *pain-soo (RRah-pee-doo)*
rash	irritação de pele *ee-RRee-tUH-souŋ dae peh-l*, brotoeja *broo-too-ae-JUH*
spot	borbulha *boor-bool-yUH*
sunburn	queimadura solar *kay-mUH-doo-rUH soo-lahr*
sunstroke	insolação *een-soo-lUH-souŋ*
surgical spirit	álcool etílico *ahl-kool ae-tee-lee-koo*
tablet	comprimido *kom-pree-mee-doo*
temperature	febre *feh-bre*
vaccination	vacina *vUH-see-nUH*
x-ray	radiografia *RRah-dee-oo-grUH-fee-ya*
to cough	tossir *too-seer*
to disinfect	desinfectar *de-zeen-feh-tahr*
to faint	desmaiar *desh-mah-yahr*
to vomit	vomitar *voo-mee-tahr*

Expressing yourself

does anyone have an aspirin/a tampon/a plaster, by any chance?
por acaso alguém tem uma aspirina/um tampão/um penso rápido?
poor UH-kah-zoo ahl-gaim taim oo-mUH UHsh-pee-ree-nUH/oom tUHm-pouŋ/oom pain-soo RRah-pee-doo?

I need to see a doctor
preciso de ir ao médico
pre-see-zoo deer ow meh-dee-koo

where can I find a doctor?
onde posso encontrar um médico?
on-d poh-soo ain-kon-trahr oom meh-dee-koo?

HEALTH

107

I'd like to make an appointment for today
queria marcar uma consulta para hoje
ke-ree-ya mUHr-kahr oo-mUH kon-sool-tUH pUH-rUH o-Je

as soon as possible
o mais cedo possível
oo my-sh sae-doo poo-see-vehl

no, it doesn't matter
não, não faz mal
noUŋ, noUŋ fahsh mahl

can you send an ambulance to ...?
pode mandar uma ambulância a ...?
poh-d mUHn-dahr oo-mUH UHm-boo-lUHn-see-ya UH ...?

I've broken my glasses
parti os meus óculos
pUHr-tee oosh mae-oosh oh-koo-loosh

I've lost a contact lens
perdi uma lente de contacto
per-dee oo-mUH lain-t dae kon-tah-too

Understanding

consultório médico	doctor's surgery
farmácia de serviço	duty pharmacy
horário de consulta/ atendimento	surgery hours
receita	prescription
sala de espera	waiting room
urgências	casualty department

não temos nenhuma vaga antes de quinta-feira
there are no available appointments until Thursday

pode ser sexta-feira às duas (horas)?
is Friday at 2pm OK?

AT THE DOCTOR'S OR THE HOSPITAL

Expressing yourself

I have an appointment with Dr ...
tenho consulta marcada com o Dr ...
tain-yo kon-sool-tUH mUHr-kah-dUH kom oo doh-tor ...

I don't feel very well
não me sinto bem
noun mae seen-too baim

I don't know what it is
não sei o que é
noun say oo ke eh

I feel very weak
sinto uma grande fraqueza
seen-too oo-mUH grUHn-d frUH-kae-zUH

I've been bitten/stung by ...
fui mordido/picado por ...
fooy mor-dee-doo/pee-kah-doo poor ...

I've got a headache/toothache/stomachache
dói-me a cabeça/os dentes/o estômago
doh-ee-mae UH kUH-bae-sUH/oosh dain-tesh/oo esh-to-mUH-goo

I've got a sore throat
dói-me a garganta
doh-ee-mae UH gUHr-gUHn-tUH

my back hurts
dói-me as costas
doh-ee-mae UHsh kohsh-tUHsh

it hurts
dói
doh-ee

it hurts here
dói-me aqui
doh-ee-mae UH-kee

I feel sick
sinto náuseas
seen-too now-zee-UHsh

it's got worse
piorou
pee-oo-ro

it's been three days
há três dias
ah traysh dee-UHsh

it started last night
começou ontem à noite
koo-mae-so on-taim ah noy-t

I have a heart condition
sofro do coração
so-froo doo koo-rUH-soun

it's never happened to me before
nunca me aconteceu
noon-kUH mae UH-kon-tae-sae-oo

I've got a temperature
tenho febre
tain-yo feh-bre

I have asthma
tenho asma
tain-yo ash-mUH

I've been on antibiotics for a week and I'm not getting any better
estou a tomar antibióticos à uma semana e não estou melhor
esh-to UH too-mahr UHn-tee-bee-oh-tee-koosh ah oo-mUH s-mUH-nUH ee noun esh-to mael-yohr

it itches
faz comichão
fahsh koo-mee-shoun

I'm ... months pregnant
estou grávida de ... meses
esh-to grah-vee-dUH dae ... mae-zesh

I'm on the pill/the minipill
tomo a pílula/a mini-pílula
toh-moo UH pee-loo-lUH/UH mee-nee pee-loo-lUH

I'm allergic to penicillin
sou alérgico/alérgica à penicilina
so UH-lehr-Jee-koo/UH-lehr-Jee-kUH ah pe-nee-see-lee-nUH

I've twisted my ankle
torci o pé
toor-see oo peh

I've had a blackout
tive uma síncope
tee-v oo-mUH seen-koo-p

I fell and hurt my back
caí e magoei as costas
kUH-ee ee mUH-goo-ay UHsh kohsh-tUHsh

I've lost a filling
perdi um chumbo/uma obturação (de um dente)
per-dee oom shoom-boo/oo-mUH ob-too-rUH-soun (doom dain-t)

is it serious?
é grave?
eh grah-v?

is it contagious?
é contagioso?
eh kon-tUH-Jee-o-zoo?

how is he/she?
como é que ele/ela está?
ko-moo eh ke ae-l/eh-lUH esh-tah?

how much do I owe you?
quanto devo?
kwUHn-too dae-voo?

can I have a receipt?
pode dar-me um recibo?
poh-d dahr-mae oom RRe-see-boo?

Understanding

aguarde na sala de espera, se faz favor
please take a seat in the waiting room

onde é que lhe dói?
where does it hurt?

respire fundo
take a deep breath

deite-se, se faz favor
lie down, please

é alérgico/alérgica a …?
are you allergic to …?

dói-lhe quando carrego/pressiono aqui?
does it hurt when I press here?

está vacinado/vacinada contra …?
have you been vaccinated against …?

está a tomar algum outro medicamento?
are you taking any other medication?

deverá passar ao fim de uns dias
it should clear up in a few days

deverá cicatrizar rapidamente
it should heal quickly

é preciso operar
you're going to need an operation

volte cá daqui a uma semana
come back and see me in a week

vou passar-lhe uma receita
I'm going to write you a prescription

AT THE CHEMIST'S

Expressing yourself

I'd like a box of plasters, please
queria uma caixa de pensos rápidos, se faz favor
ke-ree-ya oo-mUH kaee-shUH dae pain-soosh RRah-pee-doosh, s-fahsh fUH-vor

could I have something for a bad cold?
dá-me qualquer coisa para as constipações?
dah-mae kwahl-kehr koy-zUH pUH-rUH UHsh konsh-tee-pUH-soinsh?

I need something for a cough
queria qualquer coisa para a tosse
ke-ree-ya kwahl-kehr koy-zUH pUH-rUH UH toh-s

I'm allergic to aspirin
sou alérgico/alérgica à aspirina
so UH-lehr-Jee-koo/UH-lehr-Jee-kUH ah UHsh-pee-ree-nUH

I need the morning-after pill
preciso da pílula do dia seguinte
pre-see-zoo dUH pee-loo-lUH doo dee-ya se-geen-t

I'd like to try a homeopathic remedy
gostaria de tentar algo homeopático
goosh-tUH-ree-ya dae tain-tahr ahl-goo oh-mae-oh-pah-tee-koo

I'd like a bottle of solution for soft contact lenses
queria líquido para lentes de contacto moles
ke-ree-ya lee-kee-doo pUH-rUH lain-tesh dae kon-tah-too moh-lesh

Understanding

anti-inflamatório	anti-inflammatory
aplicar	apply
cápsula	capsule
contra-indicações	contra-indications
creme	cream
drageia	tablet
para uso externo	for external use only
pastilha para a garganta	throat lozenge
pó	powder
pomada	ointment
possíveis efeitos secundários	possible side effects
só com receita (médica)	available on prescription only
supositório	suppository
tomar três vezes ao dia antes das refeições	take three times a day before meals
xarope	syrup

Some informal expressions

estar de molho to be stuck in bed
estar adoentado/adoentada to feel poorly
ter um fanico to pass out
estar atacado/atacada to feel quite rough

HEALTH

PROBLEMS AND EMERGENCIES

In large towns, the police service is called the **PSP** (Polícia de Segurança Pública), while in rural areas it is the **GNR** (Guarda Nacional Republicana). **BT** (Brigada de Trânsito) is the traffic police branch of the GNR, and its officers wear red armbands.

The basics

accident	acidente *UH-see-dain-t*
ambulance	ambulância *UHm-boo-lUHn-see-ya*
broken	partido/partida *pUHr-tee-doo/pUHr-tee-dUH*
coastguard	guarda-costeira *gwahr-dUH koosh-tay-rUH*
disabled	deficiente *de-fee-see-ain-t*
doctor	médico/médica *meh-dee-koo/meh-dee-kUH*
emergency	urgência *oor-Jain-see-ya*, emergência *ee-mer-Jain-see-ya*
fire	incêndio *een-sain-dee-o*, fogo *fo-goo*
fire brigade	bombeiros *bom-bay-roosh*
hospital	hospital *ohsh-pee-tahl*
ill	doente *doo-ain-t*
injured	ferido/ferida *fe-ree-doo/fe-ree-dUH*
police	polícia *poo-lee-see-ya*

Expressing yourself

can you help me?
pode ajudar-me?
poh-d UH-Joo-dahr-mae?

help!
socorro!, ajuda!
soo-ko-RRoo!, UH-Joo-dUH!

fire!
fogo!
fo-goo!

be careful!
cuidado!
kwee-dah-doo!

it's an emergency!
é uma emergência!
eh oo-mUH ee-mer-Jain-see-ya!

there's been an accident
houve um acidente
oh-v oom UH-see-dain-t

could I borrow your phone, please?
posso utilizar o seu telefone, se faz favor?
poh-soo oo-tee-lee-zahr oo sae-oo te-le-foh-n, s-fahsh fUH-vor?

I need a doctor, quick!
preciso de um médico, depressa!
pre-see-zoo dae oom meh-dee-koo, de-preh-sUH!

what do I have to do?
o que é que tenho que fazer?
oo ke eh ke tain-yo ke fUH-zaer?

does anyone here speak English?
alguém fala inglês?
ahl-gaim fah-lUH een-glaysh?

I need to contact the British consulate
preciso de contactar o consulado britânico
pre-see-zo dae kon-tUH-tahr oo kon-soo-lah-doo bree-tUHn-nee-koo

where's the nearest police station?
onde fica a esquadra mais próxima?
on-d fee-kUH UH esh-kwah-drUH my-sh proh-see-mUH?

my passport/credit card has been stolen
o meu passaporte/cartão de crédito foi roubado
oo mae-oo pah-sUH-pohr-t/kUHr-touŋ dae kreh-dee-too foy-ee RRo-bah-doo

I've lost …
perdi …
per-dee …

my bag's been snatched
roubaram-me a carteira
RRo-bah-rUHm-mae UH kUHr-tay-rUH

I've been attacked
fui atacado/atacada
fooy-ee UH-tUH-kah-doo/UH-tUH-kah-dUH

my son/daughter is missing
o meu filho/a minha filha desapareceu
oo mae-oo feel-yo/UH meen-ya feel-yah de-zUH-pUH-re-sae-oo

my car's been towed away
o meu carro foi rebocado
oo mae-oo kah-RRoo foy-ee RRe-boo-kah-doo

I've broken down
o meu carro avariou
oo mae-oo kah-RRoo ah-vUH-ree-o

my car's been broken into
assaltaram-me o carro
UH-sahl-tah-rUHm-mae oo kah-RRoo

there's a man following me
um homem anda a seguir-me
oom oh-maim UHn-dUH ah se-geer-mae

is there disabled access?
há algum acesso especial para deficientes?
ah ahl-goom UH-seh-soo esh-pe-see-ahl pUH-rUH de-fee-see-ain-tesh?

can you keep an eye on my things for a minute?
importa-se de olhar pelas minhas coisas um minuto?
*eem-pohr-tUH-sae dae ohl-yahr pae-lUHsh meen-yas koy-zUHsh oom
mee-noo-too?*

she's not feeling well, please call a doctor/an ambulance
ela não se está a sentir bem, chamem um médico/a ambulância
*eh-lUH nouŋ sae esh-tah a sain-teer baim, shUH-maim oom meh-dee-koo/
UH UHm-boo-lUHn-see-ya*

Understanding

avariado/avariada	out of order
caixa de primeiros-socorros	first-aid box
cuidado com o cão	beware of the dog
farmácia de serviço	duty pharmacy
perdidos e achados	lost property
polícia de emergência	police emergency services
pronto-socorro	ambulance/emergency services
saída de emergência	emergency exit
serviço de reboque	breakdown service

POLICE

Expressing yourself

I want to report something stolen
queria participar um roubo
ke-ree-ya pUHr-tee-see-pahr oom RRo-boo

I need a document from the police for my insurance company
preciso de um papel da polícia para apresentar à companhia de seguros
pre-see-zo doom pUH-pehl dUH poo-lee-see-ya pUH-rUH UH-pre-zain-tahr ah kom-pUH-nee-yUHh dae se-goo-roosh

Understanding

Filling in forms

apelido/sobrenome/nome de família surname
nome (de baptismo) first name
endereço/morada address   **código postal** postcode
país country   **nacionalidade** nationality
data de nascimento date of birth
local de nascimento place of birth
idade age   **sexo** sex
duração da estadia duration of stay
data de chegada/partida arrival/departure date
profissão occupation
número de passaporte passport number

importa-se de abrir o saco?   **o que é que lhe falta?**
would you open this bag, please?   what's missing?

quando é que aconteceu?   **onde está alojado?**
when did this happen?   where are you staying?

pode descrevê-lo/descrevê-la?   **pode assinar aqui?**
can you describe him/her/it?   would you sign here, please?

importa-se de preencher esta ficha?
would you fill in this form, please?

Some informal expressions

cadeia prison
ir parar atrás das grades to go to prison/to get arrested
meter-se em/arranjar sarilhos to get into trouble

TIME AND DATE

The basics

after	depois *de-**poy**-eesh*
already	já *Jah*
always	sempre *saim-pre*
at lunchtime	à hora do almoço *ah oh-rUH doo ahl-**mo**-soo*
at the beginning/end of	no início/fim de *noo ee-**nee**-see-oo/feem dae*
at the moment	neste momento *naesh-t moo-**main**-too*
before	antes *UHn-tesh*
between ... and ...	entre as ... e as ... *ain-tre UHsh ... ee UHsh ...*
day	dia *dee-ya*
during	durante *doo-rUHn-t*
early	cedo *sae-doo*, adiantado/adiantada *UH-dee-UHn-**tah**-doo/UH-dee-UHn-**tah**-dUH*
evening	noite *noy-t*
for a long time	durante muito tempo *doo-rUHn-t mooy-too taim-poo*
from ... to ...	de ... a ... *dae ... UH ...*
from time to time	de vez em quando *dae vaysh aim kwUHn-doo*
in a little while	daqui a pouco *dUH-kee UH po-koo*
in the evening	à noite *ah noy-t*
in the middle of	no meio de *noo may-oo dae*
last	último/última *ool-tee-moo/ool-tee-mUH*
late	tarde *tahr-d*, atrasado/atrasada *UH-trUH-**sah**-doo/UH-trUH-**sah**-dUH*
midday	meio-dia *may-oo **dee**-ya*
midnight	meia-noite *may-UH noy-t*
month	mês *maysh*
morning	manhã *mUHn-**yUH***
never	nunca *noon-kUH*
next	próximo/próxima *proh-see-moo/proh-see-mUH*
night	noite *noy-t*
not yet	ainda não *UH-**een**-dUH nounη*
now	agora *UH-**goh**-rUH*
occasionally	às vezes *ahsh **vae**-zesh*
often	muitas vezes *mooy-tUHsh **vae**-zesh*

rarely	raras vezes *RRah-rUHsh vae-zesh*
recently	recentemente *re-sain-te-main-t*
since	desde *daesh-d*
sometimes	por vezes *poor vae-zesh*
soon	em breve *aim breh-v*
still	ainda *UH-een-dUH*
straightaway	imediatamente *ee-mae-dee-ah-tUH-main-t*
until	até *UH-teh*
week	semana *smUH-nUH*
weekend	fim-de-semana *feem dae smUH-nUH*
year	ano *UH-noo*

Expressing yourself

see you soon!
até breve!
UH-teh breh-v!

see you later!
até mais tarde!
UH-teh my-sh tahr-d!

see you on Monday!
até segunda!
UH-teh se-goon-dUH!

have a good weekend!
bom fim-de-semana!
bom feem dae smUH-nUH!

sorry I'm late
desculpe o atraso
desh-kool-p oo UH-trah-zoo

I haven't been there yet
ainda lá não fui
UH-een-dUH lah noun fooy

I haven't had time to ...
não tive tempo de...
noun tee-v taim-poo dae...

I've got plenty of time
tenho imenso tempo
tain-yo ee-main-soo taim-poo

I'm in a rush
estou com pressa
esh-to kom preh-sUH

hurry up!
depressa!
de-preh-sUH!

just a minute, please
espere um minuto, se faz favor
esh-peh-ree oom mee-noo-too, s-fahsh fUH-vor

I had a late night
deitei-me tarde
day-tay-m tahr-d

I got up very early
levantei-me muito cedo
le-vUHn-tay-m mooy-too sae-doo

I waited ages
estive séculos à espera
esh-*tee*-v *seh*-koo-loosh ah esh-*peh*-rUH

I have to get up very early tomorrow to catch my plane
tenho de me levantar muito cedo para apanhar o avião
tain-yo dae mae le-vUHn-*tahr mooy*-too sae-doo *pUH*-rUH UH-pUHn-*yahr*
oo UH-vee-ouŋ

we only have four days left
só temos mais quatro dias
soh *tae*-moosh *my*-sh *kwah*-troo *dee*-yash

THE DATE

How to express dates:

2 January 2006	**2 de Janeiro de 2006**
in June 2006	**em Junho de 2006**
from 2005 to 2006	**de 2005 a 2006**
100 BC	**século I (um) antes de Cristo (a. C.)**
300 AD	**século III (três) depois de Cristo (d. C.)**
nineteenth-century art	**a arte do século XIX (dezanove)**

The basics

... ago	há ... *ah* ...
in the middle of	a/no meio de *UH/noo may*-oo dae
in two days' time	daqui a/dentro de dois dias *dUH-kee UH/dain*-troo dae *doy*-eesh *dee*-yash
last night	ontem à noite *on*-taim ah *noy*-t
the day after tomorrow	depois de amanhã de-*poy*-eesh dah-mUHn-*yUH*
the day before yesterday	anteontem *UHn*-te-*on*-taim
today	hoje o-*Je*
tomorrow	amanhã ah-mUHn-*yUH*

tomorrow morning/ afternoon/evening	amanhã de manhã/à tarde/à noite *ah-mUHn-yUH* dae *mUHn-yUH*/ah *tahr-d*/ah *noy-t*
yesterday	ontem *on-taim*
yesterday morning/ afternoon/evening	ontem de manhã/à tarde/à noite *on-taim* dae *mUHn-yUH*/ah *tahr-d*/ah *noy-t*

Expressing yourself

I was born in 1975
nasci em 1975
nUHsh-see aim meel *noh-ve-sain-toosh* ee *s-tain-tUH* ee *seen-koo*

I came here a few years ago
estive cá há alguns anos
esh-tee-v kah ah ahl-*goonsh UH-noosh*

I spent a month in Portugal last summer
estive um mês em Portugal no Verão passado
esh-tee-v oom *maysh* aim poor-too-*gahl* noo ve-*roun* pUH-*sah-doo*

I was here last year at the same time
estive aqui no ano passado pela mesma altura
esh-tee-v UH-kee noo *UH-noo* pUH-*sah-doo* pae-lUH *maesh-mUH* ahl-*too-rUH*

what's the date today?
a quantos estamos?
UH kwUHn-toosh esh-*tUH-moosh?*

what day is it today?	**it's the 1st of May**
que dia é hoje?	um de Maio
ke *dee-ya* eh *o-Je?*	oom dae *mah-yo*

I'm staying until Sunday	**we're leaving tomorrow**
fico até domingo	partimos amanhã
fee-koo UH-teh doo-*meen-goo*	pUHr-*tee-moosh* ah-mUHn-*yUH*

I already have plans for Tuesday
já tenho planos para terça
Jah tain-yo plUH-noosh pUH-rUH *taer-sUH*

TIME AND DATE

Understanding

de madrugada	in the small hours/early in the morning
todas as segundas	every Monday
todos os dias	every day
três vezes por hora/por dia	three times an hour/a day
uma vez/duas vezes	once/twice

foi construído/construída em meados do século XIX
it was built in the mid-nineteenth century

no Verão tem muita gente
it gets very busy here in the summer

regressa quando?	**quanto tempo vai ficar?**
when are you leaving?	how long are you staying?

THE TIME

> **Some informal expressions**
> **à uma em ponto** at one on the dot
> **às oito e tal** after eight
> **eram umas dez e pico** it was after ten

The basics

half an hour	meia-hora *may-UH oh-rUH*
in the afternoon	à tarde *ah tahr-d*
in the morning	de manhã *dae mUHn-yUH*
midday	meio-dia *may-oo dee-ya*
midnight	meia-noite *may-UH noy-t*
on time	a horas *UH oh-rUHsh*
quarter of an hour	quarto de hora *kwahr-too doh-rUH*
three quarters of an hour	três quartos de hora *traysh kwahr-toosh doh-rUH*

Expressing yourself

what time is it?
que horas são?
*ke oh-rUHsh sou*ŋ*?*

excuse me, have you got the time, please?
desculpe, podia dizer-me as horas?
*desh-**kool**-p, poo-**dee**-ya dee-**zaer**-mae UHsh oh-rUHsh?*

it's exactly three o'clock
são três horas em ponto
*sou*ŋ *traysh oh-rUHsh aim **pon**-too*

it's nearly one o'clock
é quase uma hora
*eh **kwah**-ze oo-mUH oh-rUH*

it's ten past one
é uma e dez
*eh oo-mUH ee **deh**-sh*

it's a quarter past one
é uma e um quarto
*eh oo-mUH ee oom **kwahr**-too*

it's a quarter to one
é uma menos um quarto
*eh oo-mUH **mae**-noosh oom **kwahr**-too*

it's twenty past twelve
é meio-dia e vinte
*eh **may**-oo **dee**-ya ee **veen**-t*

it's half past one
é uma e meia
*eh oo-mUH ee **may**-UH*

it's twenty to twelve
são vinte para o meio-dia
*sou*ŋ *veen-t **pUH**-rUH oo **may**-oo **dee**-ya*

I arrived at about two o'clock
cheguei por volta das duas
*shae-**gay** poor **vohl**-tUH dash **doo**-UHsh*

I set my alarm for nine
pus o despertador para as nove
*poosh oo desh-per-t**UH**-**dor** p**UH**-rUH UHsh **noh**-v*

I waited twenty minutes
esperei vinte minutos
*esh-pe-**ray** **veen**-t mee-**noo**-toosh*

the train was fifteen minutes late/arrived on time
o comboio chegou quinze minutos atrasado/chegou à tabela
*oo kom-**boh**-yoo shae-**go** **keen**-z mee-**noo**-toosh UH-trUH-**zah**-doo/shae-**go***
*ah tUH-**beh**-lUH*

I got home an hour ago
cheguei a casa há uma hora
*shae-**gay** UH **kah**-sUH ah oo-mUH **oh**-rUH*

shall we meet in half an hour?
encontramo-nos daqui a meia-hora?
*ain-kon-**trUH**-moo-noosh dUH-**kee** UH **may**-UH **oh**-rUH?*

I'll be back in a quarter of an hour
volto daqui a um quarto de hora
***vohl**-too dUH-**kee** UH oom **kwahr**-too **doh**-rUH*

there's a three-hour time difference between … and …
há três horas de diferença entre … e …
*ah traysh **oh**-rUHsh dae dee-fae-**rain**-sUH **ain**-tree … ee …*

TIME AND DATE

Understanding

partidas todas as horas e meias-horas
departs on the hour and the half-hour

aberto entre as 10h e as 16h
open from 10am to 4pm

todas os dias às 19h
every evening at seven

dura cerca de uma hora e meia
it lasts around an hour and a half

abre às dez da manhã
it opens at ten in the morning

NUMBERS

How to write and say numbers

EUR 1 923,67   **mil novecentos e vinte e três euros e sessenta e sete cêntimos** *meel noh-ve-sain-toosh ee veen-t ee traysh aeoo-roosh ee se-sain-tUH ee seh-t sain-tee-moosh*

EUR 123   **cento e vinte e três euros** *sain-to ee veen-t ee traysh aeoo-roosh*

EUR 0,65   **sessenta e cinco cêntimos** *se-sain-tUH ee seen-koo sain-tee-moosh*

0 zero *zeh-roo*
1 um/uma *oom/oo-mUH*
2 dois/duas *doy-eesh/doo-UHsh*
3 três *traysh*
4 quatro *kwah-troo*
5 cinco *seen-koo*
6 seis *saysh*
7 sete *seh-t*
8 oito *oy-too*
9 nove *noh-v*
10 dez *deh-sh*
11 onze *on-z*
12 doze *do-z*
13 treze *trae-z*
14 catorze *kUH-tohr-z*
15 quinze *keen-z*
16 dezasseis *de-zUH-saysh*
17 dezassete *de-zUH-seh-t*
18 dezoito *de-zoy-too*
19 dezanove *de-zUH-noh-v*
20 vinte *veen-t*
21 vinte e um/uma *veen-t ee oom/oo-mUH*

22 vinte e dois/duas *veen-t ee doy-eesh/doo-UHsh*
30 trinta *treen-tUH*
35 trinta e cinco *treen-tUH ee seen-koo*
40 quarenta *kwUH-rain-tUH*
50 cinquenta *seen-kwain-tUH*
60 sessenta *se-sain-tUH*
70 setenta *s-tain-tUH*
80 oitenta *oy-tain-tUH*
90 noventa *no-vain-tUH*
100 cem *sain*
101 cento e um/uma *sain-too ee oom/oo-mUH*
200 duzentos/duzentas *doo-zain-toosh/doo-zain-tUHsh*
500 quinhentos/quinhentas *keen-yain-toosh/keen-yain-tUHsh*
1 000 mil *meel*
2 000 dois/duas mil *doy-eesh/doo-UHsh meel*
10 000 dez mil *deh-sh meel*
1 000 000 um milhão *oom meel-youŋ*

first primeiro/primeira *pree-may-roo/pree-may-rUH*
second segundo/segunda *s-goon-doo/s-goon-dUH*
third terceiro/terceira *ter-say-roo/ter-say-rUH*
fourth quarto/quarta *kwahr-too/kwahr-tUH*
fifth quinto/quinta *keen-too/keen-tUH*
sixth sexto/sexta *saysh-too/saysh-tUH*
seventh sétimo/sétima *seh-tee-moo/seh-tee-mUH*
eighth oitavo/oitava *oy-tah-voo/oy-tah-vUH*
ninth nono/nona *no-noo/no-nUH*
tenth décimo/décima *deh-see-moo/deh-see-mUH*
twentieth vigésimo/vigésima *vee-Jeh-zee-moo/vee-Jeh-zee-mUH*

20 plus 3 equals 23
vinte mais três são vinte e três
veen-t my-sh traysh souŋ veen-t ee traysh

20 minus 3 equals 17
vinte menos três são dezassete
veen-t mae-noosh traysh souŋ de-zUH-seh-t

20 multiplied by 4 equals 80
vinte vezes quatro são oitenta
veen-t vae-zesh kwah-troo souŋ oy-tain-tUH

20 divided by 4 equals 5
vinte a dividir por quatro são cinco
veen-t UH dee-vee-deer poor kwah-troo souŋ seen-koo

NUMBERS

125

DICTIONARY

ENGLISH-PORTUGUESE

A

a um *m*/uma *f* *(see grammar)*
abbey abadia *f*
able: to be able to ser capaz de
about *(approximately)* cerca de; **it takes about five minutes** demora cerca de cinco minutos; **to be about to** estar prestes a
above *(level)* acima de; *(number, quantity)* mais de; *(positioned)* por cima de, sobre; **above sea level** acima do nível do mar; **above 100 people** mais de 100 pessoas; **above the seats** sobre os/por cima dos lugares; **the floor above** o andar de cima
abroad no estrangeiro; **to go abroad** ir para o estrangeiro
accept aceitar
access acesso *m* 115
accident acidente *m* 33, 114
accommodation alojamento *m*
across do outro lado de; **the hotel across the road** o hotel do outro lado da rua; **to travel across the country** viajar pelo país; **to walk across a bridge** atravessar uma ponte
adaptor adaptador *m*
address morada *f*, endereço *m* 17
admission entrada *f*
advance: in advance adiantado *m*/adiantada *f*
advice conselho *m*
advise aconselhar
aeroplane avião *m*
after *(in time)* depois (de), após; *(in space)* atrás de; **after breakfast** depois do/após o pequeno-almoço; **one after the**

other um atrás do outro
afternoon tarde *f*
after-sun (cream) creme *m* hidratante para depois do sol
again outra vez
against contra
age idade *f*
air ar *m*
air conditioning ar-condicionado *m*
airline companhia aérea *f*
airmail correio *m* aéreo; **by airmail** por avião
airport aeroporto *m*
alarm clock despertador *m*
alcohol álcool *m*
alive vivo *m*/viva *f*
all *(everything)* tudo *m*; *(with singular noun)* todo *m*/toda *f*; *(with plural noun)* todos *mpl*/todas *fpl*; **all inclusive** tudo incluído; **all day** todo o dia; **all week** toda a semana; **all the better** tanto melhor; **all the same** de qualquer maneira; **all the time** o tempo todo
allergic alérgico *m*/alérgica *f* 111
almost quase
already já
also também
although se bem que
always sempre
ambulance ambulância *f*
American americano *m*/americana *f*
among entre
anaesthetic anestesia *f*
and e
animal animal *m*
ankle tornozelo *m*
anniversary aniversário *m*
another outro *m*/outra *f*

answer (n) resposta f
answer (v) responder
ant formiga f
antibiotic antibiótico m
anybody, anyone (in statements) qualquer um m/qualquer uma f; (in questions) alguém
anything (in statements) qualquer coisa; (in questions) alguma coisa
anyway de qualquer maneira
appendicitis apendicite f
appointment consulta f; **to make an appointment** marcar uma consulta 108; **to have an appointment (with)** ter uma consulta (com) 108
April Abril m
area área f, zona f; **in the area** na zona, na área
arm braço m
around (approximately) por volta de, cerca de; **around here/there** por aqui/aí; **around midnight** cerca da meia-noite; **I'm just looking around** estou só a ver; **to travel around the country** viajar pelo país
arrange organizar; **to arrange to meet (sb)** encontro (com alguém)
arrival chegada f
arrive chegar
art arte f
artist artista mf
as como; **as soon as possible** logo que possível; **as soon as** assim que; **as well as** bem como
ashtray cinzeiro m
ask (enquire) perguntar; (request) pedir; **to ask a question** fazer uma pergunta
aspirin aspirina f
asthma asma f
at em; **at the hotel** no hotel; **at night/2 am** à noite/às duas da manhã
attack (v) atacar 114
August Agosto m
autumn Outono m
available disponível
avenue avenida f

away: 10 miles away a dez milhas (daqui)

ß

baby bebé mf
baby's bottle biberão m
back (of person) costas fpl; (of thing) parte f de trás; **at the back of** nas traseiras de
backpack mochila f
bad (person, weather) mau m/má f; (food) estragado m/estragada f; **it's not bad** não está mal
bag (plastic, paper) saco m, saca f; (handbag) mala f
baggage bagagem f
baker's, bakery padeiro m, padaria f
balcony varanda f
ball bola f
bandage ligadura f
bank banco m 93
banknote nota f
bar (place) bar m; (counter) balcão m
barbecue churrasco m
bath banho m; (bathtub) banheira f; **to have a bath** tomar banho
bathroom casa-de-banho f
bath towel toalha f de banho
battery (of radio) pilha f; (of car) bateria f
be (referring to intrinsic quality, role) ser; (referring to changeable state) estar; (exist) haver; **I am a teacher** sou professora; **it's cold** está frio; **we are on holiday** estamos de férias; **is there a restaurant nearby?** há algum restaurante aqui perto?; **I am 25 years old** tenho 25 anos
beach praia f
beach umbrella chapéu m (de praia)
beard barba f
beautiful lindo m/linda f
because porque; **because of** por causa de
bed cama f
bee abelha f
before antes (de)

begin começar
beginner principiante *mf*
beginning início *m*; **at the beginning** no início
behind atrás (de)
believe acreditar
below *(certain level)* abaixo; *(under)* debaixo; **below zero** abaixo de zero; **the floor below** o andar de baixo
beside ao lado de, junto a
best melhor; **the best** o melhor *m*/a melhor *f*
better melhor; **to get better** melhorar; **it's better to …** é melhor …
between entre
bicycle bicicleta *f*
bicycle pump bomba *f* de bicicleta
big grande
bike bicicleta *f*
bill conta *f* **40**, **50**
bin caixote *m* do lixo
binoculars binóculos *mpl*
birthday aniversário *m*
bit pedaço *m*, bocado *m*
bird pássaro *m*
bite *(n)* *(from animal)* mordedura *f*; *(from insect)* picada *f*; *(of food)* dentada *f*
bite *(v)* *(of person, animal)* morder; *(of insect)* picar **109**
black negro *m*/negra *f*, preto *m*/preta *f*
blackout síncope *f*, desmaio *m*
blanket cobertor *m*, manta *f*
bleed sangrar
bless: bless you! santinho!
blind cego *m*/cega *f*
blister bolha *f* *(de água)*
blood sangue *m*
blood pressure tensão *f* arterial
blue azul
board *(v)* embarcar
boarding embarque *m*
boat barco *m*
body corpo *m*
book *(n)* livro *m*
book *(v)* reservar **47**, **67**
bookshop livraria *f*

boot *(shoe)* bota *f*; *(of car)* porta-bagagem *m*
boring aborrecido *m*/aborrecida *f*
borrow pedir emprestado *m*/emprestada *f*
botanical garden jardim *m* botânico
both ambos *m*/ambas *f*; **both of us** nós os dois/nós as duas
bottle garrafa *f*
bottle opener abre-garrafas *m*
bottom *(of person)* traseiro *m*; *(of thing)* fundo *m*; **at the bottom (of)** no fundo (de)
bowl tigela *f*
boy rapaz *m*
boyfriend namorado *m*
bra soutiã *m*
bracelet pulseira *f*
brake *(n)* travão *m*
brake *(v)* travar
break partir; **to break one's leg** partir a perna
break down avariar **32**, **115**
breakdown avaria *f*
breakdown service pronto-socorro *m*
breakfast pequeno-almoço *m* **39**; **to have breakfast** tomar o pequeno-almoço
bridge ponte *f*
bring trazer
brochure brochura *f*
broken partido *m*/partida *f*
bronchitis bronquite *f*
brother irmão *m*
brown castanho *m*/castanha *f*
brush escova *f*
build construir
building edifício *m*
bump *(n)* *(on head)* galo *m*; *(on arm, leg)* inchaço *m*
bumper pára-choques *m*
buoy bóia *f*
bureau de change casa *f* de câmbio
burn *(n)* queimadura *f*
burn *(v)* queimar; **to burn oneself** queimar-se
burst *(v)* rebentar
burst *(adj)* rebentado *m*/rebentada *f*

bus autocarro *m*, carreira *f* **29**
business class classe *f* executiva
bus route percurso *m*
bus station (estação) rodoviária *f*
bus stop paragem de *f* autocarro
busy *(person)* ocupado *m*/ocupada *f*; *(place, street)* movimentado *m*/movimentada *f*
but mas
butcher's talho *m*
button botão *m*
buy comprar **83**
by *(place)* a; *(means)* de; *(agent)* por; **by the window** à janela; **by the sea** à beira-mar; **by car** de carro; **made/written by** feito/escrito por
bye! adeus!, chau!

C

cable *(of appliance)* fio *m*
cable TV televisão *f* por cabo
café café *m*
call *(n)* chamada *f*, telefonema *m*
call *(v)* chamar; **to be called** chamar-se
call back *(phone)* voltar a telefonar **104**
camera máquina *f* fotográfica, câmara *f*
camper campista *mf*
camping acampar; **to go camping** acampar
camping stove fogão *m* de campismo
campsite parque *m* de campismo **43**
can *(n)* lata *f*
can *(v)* *(be able, allowed)* poder; *(know how)* saber; *(have the capacity)* conseguir; **I can't** não posso; **I can't swim** não sei nadar; **I can't sleep** não consigo dormir
cancel cancelar
candle vela *f*
can opener abre-latas *m*
car carro *m*, automóvel *m*
caravan caravana *f*
card *(for information, greetings)* cartão *m*; *(playing card)* carta *f*
car park parque *m* de estacionamento
carry levar

case: in case of ... no caso de ...
cash dinheiro *m*; **to pay cash** pagar em dinheiro **85**
cashpoint caixa *m* automático, Multibanco *m* **94**
castle castelo *m*
casualty (department) urgências *fpl*
catch apanhar
cathedral catedral *f*
CD CD *m*
cemetery cemitério *m*
centimetre centímetro *m*
centre centro *m*
century século *m*
chair cadeira *f*
chairlift telecadeira *f*
change *(n)* *(alteration)* mudança *f*; *(money)* troco *m*; *(currency exchange)* câmbio *m*
change *(v)* *(money)* trocar **93**, **94**; *(clothes, place)* mudar de
changing room cabine *f* de provas **87**
channel canal *m*
chapel capela *f*
charge *(n)* *(price)* preço *m*
charge *(v)* *(price)* cobrar
cheap barato *m*/barata *f*
check verificar
check in *(at hotel)* chegar ao hotel; *(at airport)* fazer o check-in
check-in check-in *m* **25**
check out *(v)* deixar o hotel
check out *(n)* *(in shop)* caixa *f*
cheers! saúde!
chemist's farmácia *f*
cheque cheque *m*
chest peito *m*
chess xadrez *m*
child criança *f*
chilly frio *m*/fria *f*
chimney chaminé *f*
chin queixo *m*
church igreja *f*
cigar charuto *m*
cigarette cigarro *m*

cigarette paper mortalha f, papel m para cigarros
cinema cinema m
circus circo m
city cidade f
clean (adj) limpo m/limpa f
clean (v) limpar
cliff rochedo m, falésia f
climate clima m
climbing escalada f, alpinismo m; **to go climbing** fazer escalada/alpinismo
cloakroom vestiário m
close (v) fechar, encerrar
closed fechado m/fechada f, encerrado m/encerrada f
closing time horário m de encerramento
clothes roupa f, vestuário m
club (disco) discoteca f
clutch (n) (of car) embraiagem f
coach (bus) autocarro m; (on train) carruagem f
coast costa f
coathanger cabide m
cockroach barata f
coil (contraceptive) DIU m
coin moeda f
cold (n) (low temperature) frio m; (illness) constipação f; **to have a cold** estar constipado m/constipada f
cold (adj) frio m/fria f; **it's cold** está frio; **I'm cold** tenho frio
collection colecção f
colour cor f; **colour film** rolo m a cores
comb (n) pente m
come vir
come back regressar
come in entrar
come out sair
comfortable confortável
company companhia f
compartment compartimento m
complain reclamar
comprehensive insurance seguro m contra todos os riscos
computer computador m
concert concerto m **67**

concert hall sala f de concertos
concession desconto m **23**, **73**
condom preservativo m
confirm confirmar **26**
connection ligação f **26**
constipated com prisão de ventre
consulate consulado m
contact (n) contacto m
contact (v) contactar **114**
contact lenses lentes fpl de contacto
contagious contagioso m/contagiosa f
contraceptive anticoncepcional m
cook (v) cozinhar
cooking cozinhar; **to do the cooking** cozinhar
cool fresco m/fresca f
copy (n) cópia f
corkscrew saca-rolhas m
correct (adj) correcto m/correcta f
cost (v) custar
cottage vivenda f
cotton algodão m
cotton bud cotonete m
cotton wool algodão m
cough (n) tosse f; **to have a cough** ter tosse
cough (v) tossir
count contar
country país m
countryside campo m
course: of course claro, com certeza
cover (n) (of jar) tampa f; (of book) capa f
cover (v) cobrir
credit card cartão m de crédito **38**, **40**, **50**, **85**, **94**
cross (n) cruz f
cross (v) (street) atravessar
cruise cruzeiro m
cry (v) chorar
cup chávena f
currency moeda f
customs alfândega f
cut cortar; **to cut oneself** cortar-se
cycle path percurso m para bicicletas **80**
cycling ciclismo m

D

damaged danificado m/danificada f
damp húmido m/húmida f
dance (n) dança f
dance (v) dançar
dangerous perigoso m/perigosa f
dark escuro m/escura f; **dark blue** azul-escuro
date (n) data f; **out of date** desactualizado m/desactualizada f
date (from) datado m/datada f (de)
date of birth data f de nascimento
daughter filha f
day dia m; **the day after tomorrow** depois de amanhã; **the day before yesterday** anteontem
dead morto m/morta f
deaf surdo m/surda f
dear querido m/querida f
debit card cartão m de débito
December Dezembro m
declare declarar
deep profundo m/profunda f
degree (level) grau m
delay atraso m
delayed atrasado m/atrasada f
deli charcutaria f
dentist dentista mf
deodorant desodorizante m
department departamento m
department store grande loja f, armazém m
departure partida f
depend: that depends (on) depende (de)
deposit depósito m
dessert sobremesa f **48**
develop: to get a film developed mandar revelar um rolo (de fotografias) **91**
diabetes diabetes mpl
dialling code indicativo m
diarrhoea: to have diarrhoea ter diarreia
die (v) morrer
diesel gasóleo m

diet dieta f; **to be on a diet** estar de dieta
different (from) diferente (de)
difficult difícil
digital camera máquina f digital, câmara f digital
dinner jantar m; **to have dinner** jantar
direct directo m/directa f
direction direcção f; **to have a good sense of direction** orientar-se bem
directory lista f telefónica
directory enquiries informações fpl
dirty (adj) sujo m/suja f
disabled deficiente **115**
disaster desastre m
disco discoteca f
discount desconto m **73**; **to give someone a discount** fazer um desconto a alguém
discount fare tarifa f reduzida
dish prato m; **dish of the day** prato do dia
dishes (crockery) louça f; **to do the dishes** lavar a louça
dish towel pano m da louça
dishwasher máquina f de lavar louça
disinfect desinfectar
disposable descartável
disturb incomodar; **do not disturb** não incomodar
dive (underwater) mergulhar
diving: to go diving fazer mergulho
do fazer; **do you have a light?** tem lume?
doctor médico m/médica f **107, 114**
door porta f
door code código m da porta
downstairs andar m de baixo; **I live downstairs** moro no andar de baixo; **to go/come downstairs** descer; **the downstairs windows** as janelas do andar de baixo
dress: to get dressed vestir-se
dressing (for wound) penso m
drink (n) bebida f; **to go for a drink** ir beber um copo **46**; **to have a drink** beber um copo

drink (v) beber
drinking water água f potável
drive: to go for a drive ir dar uma volta de carro
drive (v) conduzir
driving licence carta f de condução
drops gotas fpl
drown afogar-se
drugs (illegal) drogas fpl; (medicine) medicamentos mpl
drunk bêbedo m/bêbeda f
dry (adj) seco m/seca m
dry (v) secar
dry cleaner's lavandaria-a-seco f
duck pato f
dummy chupeta f
during durante; **during the week** durante a semana
dustbin caixote m do lixo
duty chemist's farmácia f de serviço

E

each cada; **each one** cada um
ear orelha f
earache dor f de ouvidos
early cedo
earplugs tampões mpl para os ouvidos
earrings brincos mpl
earth terra f
east este m, leste m; **in the east** no este/leste; **(to the) east of** a este/leste de
Easter Páscoa f
easy fácil
eat comer **46**
economy class classe f económica
Elastoplast® adesivo m
electric eléctrico m/eléctrica m
electricity electricidade f
electricity meter contador m da electricidade
electric shaver máquina f de barbear
e-mail (n) e-mail m, correio m electrónico **99**
e-mail: to e-mail someone enviar um e-mail a aguém

e-mail address endereço m de e-mail **99**
embassy embaixada f
emergency emergência f **114**; **in an emergency** em caso de emergência
emergency exit saída f de emergência
empty vazio m/vazia m
end fim m, final m; **at the end of** no fim/final de; **at the end of the street** ao fundo da rua
engaged (phone) ocupado m/ocupada f; (to be married) noivo m/noiva f
engine motor m
England Inglaterra f
English inglês m/inglesa f; **English** (n) (language) inglês m
enjoy gostar; **enjoy your meal!** bom apetite!; **to enjoy oneself** divertir-se
enough suficiente; **that's enough** chega
en-suite com casa-de-banho privativa
entrance entrada f
envelope envelope m
epileptic epiléptico m/epiléptica f
equipment equipamento m
euro euro m
Eurocheque Eurocheque m
Europe Europa f
European europeu m/europeia f
evening noite f; **in the evening** à noite
every todos mpl/todas fpl; **every day** todos os dias; **every week** todas as semanas
everybody, everyone toda a gente, todos
everywhere em todo o lado
except excepto
excess excesso m
exchange trocar
exchange rate taxa f de câmbio
excuse (n) desculpa f
excuse: excuse me desculpe
exhaust esgotar
exhausted exausto m/exausta f
exhaust pipe cano m/tubo m de escape
exhibition exposição f **72**, **73**
exit saída f
expensive caro m/cara f
expiry date data f de validade

express *(adj)* expresso *m*/expressa *f*
expresso bica *f*, café *m*
extra extra
eye olho *m*

F

face cara *f*
facecloth toalha *f* de rosto
fact facto *m*; **in fact** de facto
faint desmaiar
fair *(n)* feira *f*
fall *(v)* cair; **to fall asleep** adormecer
family família *f*
fan *(electric)* ventoinha *f*, ventilador *m*
far longe; **far from** longe de
fare bilhete *m*
fast rápido *m*/rápida *f*
fast-food restaurant restaurante *m* de
  comida rápida
fat gordo *m*/gorda *f*
father pai *m*
favour favor *m*; **to do someone a**
  favour fazer um favor a alguém
favourite favorito *m*/favorita *f*
fax fax *m*
February Fevereiro *m*
fed up: to be fed up (with) estar farto
  m/farta *f* (de)
feel sentir; **to feel good/bad** sentir-se
  bem/mal
feeling sentimento *m*
ferry ferry *m*, barco *m*
festival festa *f* *(local)*
fetch: to go and fetch someone/
  something ir buscar alguém/alguma
  coisa
fever febre *f*; **to have a fever** ter febre
few poucos *mpl*/poucas *fpl*; **a few** alguns
  mpl/algumas *fpl*; **quite a few** bastantes
fiancé noivo *m*
fiancée noiva *f*
fight *(n)* briga *f*
file ficheiro *m*
fill encher
fill in, fill out *(form)* preencher

fill up *(petrol tank)* atestar
filling *(in tooth)* chumbo *m*, obturação *f*
film *(for camera)* rolo *m*; *(movie)* filme *m* **91**
finally por último, *(at last)* finalmente
find encontrar
fine *(n)* multa *f*
fine *(adv)* bem; **I'm fine** estou bem
finger dedo *m*
finish *(n)* acabar
fire *(n)* incêndio *m*, fogo *m*; **fire!** fogo!
fire brigade bombeiros *mpl*
fireworks fogo *m* de artifício
first primeiro *m*/primeira *f*; **first (of all)**
  primeiro, antes de mais
first class primeira classe *f*
first floor primeiro andar *m*
first name nome *m* de baptismo,
  primeiro nome *m*
fish *(n)* peixe *m*
fishmonger's peixaria *f*
fitting room cabine *f* de provas
fizzy gaseificado *m*/gaseificada *f*
flash flash *m*
flask *(Thermos®)* termo *m*
flat *(adj)* *(level)* plano *m*/plana *f*; *(battery)*
  descarregado *m*/descarregada *f*; **flat tyre**
  pneu *m* furado
flat *(n)* apartamento *m*
flavour sabor *m*
flaw defeito *m*
flight voo *m*
flip-flops chinelos *mpl* de dedo
floor *(of room)* chão *m*; *(storey)* andar *m*;
  on the floor no chão
flippers barbatanas *fpl*
flu gripe *f*
fly *(n)* mosca *f*
fly *(v)* voar
fog nevoeiro *m*
food comida *f* **85**
food poisoning intoxicação *f* alimentar
foot pé *m*, *(on foot)* a pé
for para; *(time)* durante; **for an hour**
  durante uma hora
forbidden proibido *m*/proibida *f*
forecast previsão *f*

forehead testa *f*
foreign estrangeiro *m*/estrangeira *f*
foreigner estrangeiro *m*/estrangeira *f*
forest floresta *f*
fork garfo *m*
forward *(adv)* para a frente; **to move forward** andar para a frente, avançar
forward *(adj)* *(in front)* da frente
four-star petrol gasolina *f* super
fracture fractura *f*
fragile frágil
free *(unoccupied, unrestrained)* livre; *(with no charge)* grátis, de graça
freezer congelador *m*
Friday sexta-feira *f*
fridge frigorífico *m*
friend amigo *m*/amiga *f*
from de; **from … to …** de … a …
front frente *f*; **in front of** em/à frente de; **in front of me/us** à minha/nossa frente
frying pan sertã *f*, frigideira *f*
full cheio *m*/cheia *f*; **full of** cheio/cheia de
full board pensão *f* completa
full fare, full price tarifa *f* normal, preço *m* normal
funfair feira *f* popular
fuse fusível *m*

G

gallery galeria *f* de arte
game jogo *m*
garage *(for repair)* oficina *f* **32**; *(for parking)* garagem *f*
garden jardim *m*
gas gás *m*
gas cylinder botija *f* de gás
gastric flu gripe *f* gástrica
gate *(in airport)* porta *f* de embarque; *(in garden)* portão *m*
gauze gaze *f*
gay gay, homossexual
gearbox caixa *f* de velocidades
general geral
gents' (toilet) WC *m* dos homens
get *(train, bus, illness)* apanhar; *(obtain)*

obter; *(receive)* receber; *(fetch)* ir buscar; *(become)* ficar; *(arrive)* chegar
get off *(bus)* descer
get up levantar-se
gift-wrap embrulhar para prenda **89**
girl rapariga *f*
girlfriend *(female friend)* amiga *f*; *(partner)* namorada *f*
give dar
give back devolver
glass copo *m*; **a glass of water/of wine** um copo de água/de vinho
glasses óculos *mpl*
gluten-free sem glúten
gloves luvas *fpl*
go ir; **to go to Lisbon/to Portugal** ir a Lisboa/a Portugal; **we're going home tomorrow** regressamos a casa amanhã
go away ir-se embora
goggles óculos *mpl* (protectores)
go in entrar
go out sair
go with ir com
golf golfe *m*
golf course campo *m* de golfe
good bom *m*/boa *f*; **good morning** bom dia; **good afternoon** boa tarde; **good evening** boa noite
goodbye adeus
goodnight boa noite
GP clínico *m* geral
grams gramas *mpl*
grass *(plant)* erva *f*; *(lawn)* relva *f*
great *(very good)* óptimo *m*/óptima *f*, espetacular
Great Britain Grã-Bretanha *f*
green verde
grey cinzento *m*/cinzenta *f*
grocer's mercearia *f*, minimercado *m*
ground solo *m*; **on the ground** no solo
ground floor rés-do-chão *m*
ground sheet lona *f* (para o chão)
group grupo *m*
grow crescer
guarantee garantia *f*
guest hóspede *mf*

guest house pensão f
guide (person) guia mf
guidebook guia m
guided tour visita f guiada
gynaecologist ginecologista mf

H

hair (on head) cabelo m; (body, animal) pêlo m
hairdresser cabeleireiro m/cabeleireira f
hairdryer secador m de cabelo
half metade f; **half a litre/kilo** meio litro/quilo; **half an hour** meia-hora
half-board meia-pensão f
half-pint: a half-pint um fino
hand mão m
handbag carteira f, mala f
handbrake travão m de mão
handicapped deficiente
handkerchief lenço m (da mão)
hand luggage bagagem f de mão
hand-made feito m/feita f à mão
hangover ressaca f
happen acontecer
happy feliz
hard (not soft) duro m/dura f; (difficult) difícil
hashish haxixe m
hat chapéu m; (cap) boné m
hate (v) detestar
have ter
have to ter de; **I have to go** tenho de ir
hay fever febre f dos fenos
he ele
head cabeça f
headache: to have a headache ter dor de cabeça
headlight farol m (dianteiro)
health saúde f
hear ouvir
heart coração m
heart attack ataque m cardíaco
heat (n) calor m
heating aquecimento m
heavy pesado m/pesada f

hello olá
helmet capacete m
help (n) ajuda f; **to call for help** pedir ajuda; **help!** socorro!, ajuda!
help (v) ajudar **113**
her (adj) dela; **her luggage** a bagagem dela; **her friends** os amigos dela
her (pron) (direct object) a; (indirect object) lhe; (after preposition) ela; **I know her** eu conheço-a; **I asked her** perguntei-lhe; **for her** para ela (see grammar)
here aqui; **here is/are** aqui está/estão
hers dela; **a friend of hers** um amigo dela; **they are hers** são dela; **hers are here** os/as dela estão aqui (see grammar)
herself (reflexive) se; (after preposition) ela (própria); **she hurt herself** ela magoou-se; **she didn't hurt herself** ela não se magoou (see grammar)
hi! olá!
hi-fi aparelhagem f
high alto m/alta f
high blood pressure tensão f alta
high tide maré-alta f
hiking caminhar **78**; **to go hiking** caminhar, fazer caminhada
hill monte m
hill-walking caminhar; **to go hill-walking** caminhar pelos montes
him (direct object) o; (indirect object) lhe; (after preposition) ele; **I know him** eu conheço-o; **I asked him** perguntei-lhe; **for him** para ele (see grammar)
himself (reflexive) se; (after preposition) ele (próprio); **he hurt himself** ele magoou-se; **he didn't hurt himself** ele não se magoou (see grammar)
hip anca f
hire (n) aluguer m
hire (v) (car, bike) alugar **33**, **77**, **79**
his dele; **his luggage** a bagagem dele; **his friends** os amigos dele; **a friend of his** um amigo dele; **they are his** são dele; **his are here** os/as dele estão aqui (see grammar)
hitchhike pedir boleia

hitchhiking viajar à boleia
hold *(retain, contain)* segurar;
   (party, meeting) organizar; **hold on!** *(on
   the phone)* não desligue!
holiday(s) férias *fpl*; **on holiday** de
   férias **15**
holiday camp campo *m* de férias
Holland Países *mpl* Baixos
home casa *f*; **at home** em casa; **to go
   home** voltar para casa
homosexual homossexual
honest honesto *m*/honesta *f*
honeymoon lua-de-mel *f*
horse cavalo *m*
hospital hospital *m*
hot quente; **the soup is hot** a sopa está
   quente; **a hot drink** uma bebida quente;
   it is hot *(weather)* está calor
hot chocolate chocolate *m* quente
hotel hotel *m*
hotplate placa *f* eléctrica
hour hora *f*; **an hour and a half** uma
   hora e meia
house casa *f*
housework lida *f* da casa; **to do the
   housework** encarregar-se da lida da casa
how como; **how are you?** como está?
hungry: to be hungry ter fome
hurry: to be in a hurry ter pressa
hurry (up) despachar-se, apressar-se
hurt doer; **my head hurts** dói-me a
   cabeça; **it hurts** dói **109**
husband marido *m*

I

I eu; **I'm English** sou inglês/inglesa; **I'm
   22 (years old)** tenho 22 anos
ice gelo *m*
ice cube cubo *m* de gelo
identity card bilhete *m* de identidade
identity papers identificação *f*
if se
ill doente
illness doença *f*
important importante

in em; **in England/2006/Portuguese**
   em Inglaterra/2006/português; **in the
   19th century** no século dezanove; **in
   an hour** numa hora
included incluído *m*/incluída *f*
independent independente
indicator indicador *m*
infection infecção *f*
information informação *f* **71**
injection injecção *f*
injured ferido *m*/ferida *f*
insect insecto *m*
insecticide insecticida *m*
inside *(interior)* interior; **what's inside?**
   o que tem dentro? **they're inside** estão
   lá dentro
insomnia insónia *f*
instant coffee café *m* solúvel
instead: instead of em vez de
interesting interessante
insurance seguro *m* **33**
intend to tencionar
international internacional
international money order
   transferência *f* bancária (internacional)
Internet Internet *f*
Internet café cibercafé *m*, Internet café
   m **99**
invite convidar
Ireland Irlanda *f*
Irish irlandês *m*/irlandesa *f*
iron *(n)* *(for ironing)* ferro *m* de passar
iron *(v)* passar a ferro
island ilha *f*
it ele *m*/ela *f*; **it's beautiful** é bonito; **it's
   warm** está quente
itchy: it's itchy faz comichão
item *(on bill)* parcela *f*; *(product)* artigo *m*

J

jacket casaco *m*
January Janeiro *m*
jetlag cansaço *m* provocado pela diferença
   horária
jeweller's joalharia *f*

jewellery jóias *fpl*
job emprego *m*
jogging jogging *m*
journey viagem *f*
jug jarra *f*
juice sumo *m*
July Julho *m*
jumper camisola *f*
June Junho *m*
just *(only)* apenas, só; **just a little** só um pouquinho; **just before** um pouco antes; **just one** só/apenas um; **I've just arrived** acabei de chegar; **just in case** pelo sim pelo não

K

kayak caiaque *m*
keep manter; *(change)* ficar com
key chave *f* **33**, **40**, **42**; *(of keyboard)* tecla *f*
keyboard teclado *m*
kidney rim *m*
kill matar
kilo quilo *m*
kilometre quilómetro *m*
kind *(n)* tipo *m*; **what kind of …?** que tipo de …?
kitchen cozinha *f*
knee joelho *m*
knife faca *f*
knock down derrobar
know *(fact)* saber; *(person)* conhecer; **I don't know** não sei

L

ladies' (toilet) WC *m* das Senhoras
lake lago *m*
lamp candeeiro *m*
landmark ponto *m* de referência
landscape paisagem *f*
language linguagem *f*
laptop computador *m* portátil
last *(adj)* último *m*/última *f*; **last year/month** no ano/mês passado
last *(v)* durar

late atrasado *m*/atrasada *f*, tarde **65**; **it's late, I should go** já é tarde, preciso de ir
late-night opening aberto *m*/aberta *f* até tarde
laugh *(v)* rir
launderette lavandaria *f*
lawyer advogado *m*/advogada *f*
leaflet folheto *m*
leak *(n)* *(petrol, gás)* fuga *f*; *(in roof)* goteira *f*
learn aprender
least: at least pelo menos; **the least** o/a menos
leave *(v)* partir
left esquerdo *m*/esquerda *f*; **to the left (of)** à esquerda (de)
left-luggage (office) depósito *m* de bagagem
leg perna *f*
lend emprestar
lens lente *f*
less menos; **less than** menos de
let *(allow)* deixar; *(rent out)* alugar; **let's go!** vamos!
letter carta *f*
letterbox caixa *f* do correio, marco *m* do correio
library biblioteca *f*
life vida *m*
lift elevador *m*
light *(adj)* *(in weight)* leve; *(in colour)* claro *m*/clara *f*; **light blue** azul-claro
light *(n)* luz *f*; **do you have a light?** tem lume?
light *(v)* acender
light bulb lâmpada *f*
lighter isqueiro *m*
lighthouse farol *m*
like *(adv)* como
like *(v)* gostar (de); **I'd like …** queria … **18**
line linha *f* **29**
lip lábio *m*
listen ouvir
listings magazine guia *m* de espectáculos
litre litro *m*

little *(adj)* *(time, quantity)* pouco m/pouca f; *(size, age)* pequeno m/pequena f
little *(adv)* pouco
live *(v)* viver
liver fígado m
living room sala f de estar
local time hora f local
lock *(n)* *(of door)* fechadura f; *(of suitcase)* fecho m
lock *(v)* fechar à chave
locker cacifo m
long longo m/longa f; *(hair)* comprido m/comprida f; **a long time** muito tempo; **how long … ?** quanto tempo …?; **it's one metre long** tem um metro de comprimento
look *(v)* olhar; *(seem)* parecer; **to look tired** ter ar de cansado m/cansada f
look after cuidar de
look at olhar para
look for procurar
look like parecer-se com
lorry camião m
lose perder 114; **to get lost** perder-se; **to be lost** estar perdido m/perdida f
lot: a lot (of) *(money, wine)* muito (de); *(things, people)* muitos mpl/muitas fpl (de)
loud *(noise, voice)* alto m/alta f
love *(v)* adorar
low baixo m/baixa f
low blood pressure tensão f baixa
low-fat com baixo teor de gordura
low tide maré-baixa f
luck sorte f
luggage bagagem f 26
lukewarm morno m/morna f
lunch almoço m; **to have lunch** almoçar
lung pulmão m
luxury *(n)* luxo m
luxury *(adj)* de luxo

M

magazine revista f
maiden name nome m de solteira
mail correio m

main principal
make fazer
man homem m
manage *(cope)* conseguir; **to manage to do something** conseguir fazer alguma coisa
manager gerente mf
many muitos mpl/muitas fpl; **how many?** quantos?; **how many times …?** quantas vezes …?
map mapa m 11, 28, 65, 71
March Março m
marina marina f
market mercado m 86
married casado m/casada f
mass *(religious)* missa f
match *(for fire)* fósforo m; *(game)* jogo m
material material m
matter: it doesn't matter não faz mal
mattress colchão m
May Maio m
maybe talvez
me me; *(after preposition)* mim; **don't tell me** não me digas; **he knows me** ele conhece-me; **it's for me** é para mim; **me too** eu também; **he's with me** ele está comigo (see grammar)
meal refeição f
mean significar; **what does … mean?** o que significa …?
medicine medicamento m
medium *(adj)* médio m/média f
meet encontrar 65
meeting reunião f
member membro m
menu ementa f
message mensagem f 103
meter *(for gas, electricity)* contador m
metre metro m
microwave microondas m
midday meio-dia m
middle meio m; **in the middle (of)** no meio (de)
midnight meia-noite f
might ser possível; **it might rain** é possível que chova
mill moinho m

mind *(v)* importar-se; **I don't mind** não me importo

mine o(s) meu(s)/a(s) minha(s); **a friend of mine** um amigo meu; **these are mine** estes são meus; **mine are here** os meus/as minhas estão aqui *(see grammar)*

minister *(of church)* pastor *m*

minute minuto *m*; **at the last minute** à última da hora

mirror espelho *m*

Miss Sra.

miss *(flight, train)* perder **26, 29**; *(not hit)* falhar; *(be absent)* faltar; **we missed the train** perdemos o comboio; **there are two people missing** faltam duas pessoas

mistake erro *m*; **to make a mistake** enganar-se

mobile (phone) telemóvel *m*

modern moderno *m*/moderna *f*

moisturizer creme *m* hidratante

moment momento *m*; **at the moment** no momento

monastery mosteiro *m*

Monday segunda-feira *f*

money dinheiro *m* **84**

month mês *m*

monument monumento *m*

moon lua *f*

moped motocicleta *f*

more mais; **more than** mais de; **much more, a lot more** muito mais; **there's no more** ... já não há ...

morning manhã *f*

morning-after pill pílula *f* do dia seguinte

mosque mesquita *f*

mosquito mosquito *m*

most: the most o/a mais; **most people** a maioria das pessoas

mother mãe *f*

motorbike moto *f*

motorway auto-estrada *f*

mountain montanha *f*

mountain bike bicicleta *f* de montanha

mountain hut refúgio *m* de montanha

mouse rato *m*

mouth boca *f*

move *(v)* mover; *(oneself)* mover-se

movie filme *m*

Mr Sr.

Mrs Sra.

much: how much? quanto?; **how much does it cost?** quanto custa?

muscle músculo *m*

museum museu *m*

music música *f*

must *(obligation)* ter; *(certainty)* dever; **it must be 5 o'clock** devem ser cinco horas; **I must go** tenho de ir

my o(s) meu(s)/a(s) minha(s); **that's my seat** esse é o meu lugar *(see grammar)*

myself *(reflexive)* me; *(after preposition)* mim *(próprio m/própria f)*; **I hurt myself** magoei-me; **I didn't hurt myself** não me magoei *(see grammar)*

N

nail *(of finger, toe)* unha *f*

naked nu *m*/nua *f*

name nome *m*; **my name is ...** chamo-me ...

nap soneca *f*; **to have a nap** dormir uma soneca

napkin guardanapo *m*

nappy fralda *f*

national holiday feriado *m* nacional

nature natureza *f*

near perto; **near the beach** perto da praia; **the nearest ...** o/a ... mais perto

necessary necessário *m*/necessária *f*

neck pescoço *m*

necklace colar *m*

need *(v)* precisar (de)

needle agulha *f*

neighbour vizinho *m*/vizinha *f*

neither: neither do I eu também não; **neither ... nor ...** nem ... nem ...

nervous nervoso *m*/nervosa *f*

never nunca

new novo *m*/nova *f*

news notícia *f*

newsagent quiosque *m* de jornais
newspaper jornal *m*
newsstand quiosque *m* de jornais
New Year Ano *m* Novo
next próximo *m*/próxima *f*; **next to …** junto a …, ao lado de …; **I go next** a seguir sou eu
nice *(pleasant)* agradável; *(pretty)* bonito *m*/bonita *f*; *(kind)* simpático *m*/simpática *f*
night noite *f* **39**
nightclub clube *m* nocturno
nightdress camisa *f* de noite
no não; **no, thank you** não, obrigado *m*/obrigada *f*; **no idea** não faço ideia
nobody ninguém
noise barulho *m*, ruído *m*; **to make a noise** fazer barulho/ruído
noisy barulhento *m*/barulhenta *f*, ruidoso *m*/ruidosa *f*
non-drinking water água *f* não potável
none nenhum *m*/nenhuma *f*
non-smoker não-fumador *m*/não-fumadora *f*
noon meio-dia *m*
north norte *m*; **in the north** no norte; **(to the) north of …** a norte de …
nose nariz *m*
not não; **not yet** ainda não; **not at all** *(reply to thanks)* de nada
note nota *m*
notebook bloco *m* de apontamentos
nothing nada
novel romance *m*
November Novembro *m*
now agora
nowadays hoje em dia
nowhere em lugar nenhum
number número *m*
nurse enfermeiro *m*/enfermeira *f*

obvious óbvio *m*/óbvia *f*
ocean oceano *m*
o'clock: one o'clock uma hora; **three o'clock** três horas

October Outubro *m*
of de
offer *(v)* oferecer
often muitas vezes
oil óleo *m*
ointment pomada *f*
OK ok
old velho *m*/velha *f*; **how old are you?** quantos anos tem?; **old people** os idosos
old town parte *f* antiga da cidade, zona *f* histórica
on *(prep) (position, location)* em; *(about)* sobre; **it's on at …** começa às …; **on Sunday** no domingo; **on holiday** de férias; **on foot** a pé; **on TV/the radio** na televisão/no rádio
on *(adj) (TV, light)* ligado *m*/ligada *f*
once uma vez; **once a day/an hour** uma vez por dia/por hora
one um *m*/uma *f*
only apenas
open *(adj)* aberto *m*/aberta *f*
open *(v)* abrir
operate operar
operation: to have an operation ser operado *m*/operada *f*
opinion opinião *f*; **in my opinion** na minha opinião
opportunity oportunidade *f*
opposite *(adj)* contrário *m*/contrária *f*
opposite *(prep)* em frente a
optician oculista *m*
or ou
orange laranja *f*
orchestra orquestra *f*
order *(n) (in restaurant)* pedido *m*; **out of order** fora de serviço, avariado
order *(v) (in restaurant)* pedir **48**
organic orgânico *m*/orgânica *f*
organize organizar
other outro *m*/outra *f*
otherwise *(or else)* senão; *(differently)* de outro modo
our o(s) nosso(s)/a(s) nossa(s); **those are our seats** esses são os nossos lugares *(see grammar)*

ours nosso(s)/nossa(s); **a friend of ours** um amigo nosso; **they are ours** são nossos/nossas; **ours are here** os nossos/as nossas estão aqui *(see grammar)*

ourselves *(reflexive)* nos; *(after preposition)* nós (próprios *mpl*/próprias *fpl*); **we hurt ourselves** magoámo-nos; **we didn't hurt ourselves** não nos magoámos *(see grammar)*

outside *(exterior)* exterior *m*; **can we sit outside?** podemos sentar-nos lá fora?

outward journey ida *f*

oven forno *m*

over: over there ali

overdone demasiado passado *m*/passada *f*

overweight: my luggage is overweight a minha bagagem tem excesso de peso

owe dever

own *(adj)* próprio *m*/própria *f*; **my own car** o meu próprio carro

own *(v)* possuir

owner dono *m*/dona *f*

P

pack *(v)* *(suitcase)* fazer a mala

package holiday férias *fpl* com tudo incluído

packed *(busy)* à pinha, cheio *m*/cheia *f*

packet pacote *m*; **a packet of cigarettes** um maço de cigarros

painting *(picture)* quadro *m*, *(art)* pintura *f*

pair par *m*; **a pair of shoes** um par de sapatos; **a pair of pyjamas** um pijama; **a pair of shorts** uns calções

pain dor *f*

painkiller comprimido *m* para as dores, analgésico *m*

palace palácio *m*

pants cuecas *fpl*

paper papel *m*; **paper napkin** guardanapo *m* de papel

parcel encomenda *f*

pardon? perdão?

parents pais *mpl*

park *(n)* parque *m*

park *(v)* estacionar 31

parking space lugar *m* para estacionamento

part parte *f*; **to be a part of** fazer parte de

party festa *f*

pass *(n)* passe *m*

pass *(v)* passar

passenger passageiro *m*/passageira *f*

passport passaporte *m*

past *(further than)* depois de; **a quarter past ten** dez e um quarto

past *(n)* passado *m*

path trilho *m* 79

patient doente *mf*

pay pagar 40, 85

pedestrian pediatra *mf*

pedestrianized street rua *f* pedonal

pee fazer chichi, mijar

peel *(v)* descascar

pen caneta *f*

pencil lápis *f*

people gente *f*

percent por cento

perfect perfeito *m*/perfeita *f*

perfume perfume *m*

perhaps talvez

period período *m*

person pessoa *f*

personal stereo Walkman® *m*

pet animal *m* de companhia

petrol gasolina *f* 32

petrol station posto *m* de gasolina

phone *(n)* telefone *m*

phone *(v)* telefonar

phone box cabine *f* telefónica 102

phone call telefonema *m*, chamada *f*; **to make a phone call** fazer um telefonema/uma chamada

phonecard cartão *m* telefónico 102

phone number número *m* de telefone

photo fotografia *f* 91, 92; **to take a photo (of)** tirar uma fotografia (de); **to take someone's photo** tirar uma fotografia a alguém

picnic piquenique m; **to have a picnic** fazer um piquenique

piece (bit) pedaço m; (of device, machine) peça f; **a piece of …** um pedaço de …; **a piece of fruit** uma peça de fruta

piles hemorróidas fpl

pill pílula f; **to be on the pill** tomar a pílula

pillow almofada f

pillowcase fronha f

PIN (number) código m pessoal

pink cor-de-rosa

pity: it's a pity é uma pena

place lugar m

plan (n) plano m

plane avião m

plant planta f

plaster (cast) gesso m

plastic (n) plástico m

plastic bag saca f de plástico

plate prato m

platform plataforma f; (for train) linha f **29**

play (n) peça f de teatro

play (v) (sport, game) jogar; (instrument) tocar; (of children) brincar

please se faz favor, por favor

pleased satisfeito m/satisfeita f; **pleased to meet you!** muito prazer!

pleasure prazer m

plug (on appliance) tomada f; (for bath, sink) tampa f

plug in ligar

plumber canalizador m

point (n) ponto m

police polícia f

policeman polícia m

police station esquadra f de polícia **114**

policewoman polícia f

poor pobre

port porto m

portrait retrato m

Portugal Portugal m

Portuguese português m/portuguesa f; (language) português m

possible possível

post (n) correio m

postbox marco m do correio, caixa f do correio **96**

postcard postal m

postcode código m postal

poster póster m

postman carteiro m

post office estação f de correios **96**

pot (for cooking) panela f; (for tea, coffee) bule m; (jar) frasco m

pound (currency) libra f

powder pó m

practical prático m/prática f

pram carrinho m de bebé

prefer preferir

pregnant grávida f

prepare preparar

present (n) presente m **89**

press (v) carregar, pressionar

pressure pressão f

pretty bonito m/bonita f

previous anterior

price preço m

primary school escola f primária

print (v) imprimir

private privado m/privada f

prize prémio m

probably provavelmente

problem problema m

procession procissão f

product produto m

profession profissão f

programme programa m

promise (v) prometer

propose propor

protect proteger

proud (of) orgulhoso m/orgulhosa f (de)

public (adj) público m/pública f; **public school** escola f privada

public holiday feriado m

pull puxar

purple roxo m/roxa f

purpose: on purpose de propósito

purse carteira f

push empurrar

pushchair carrinho m de bebé

put pôr

put out (light, fire) apagar
put up (tent) montar; (provide accommodation) alojar
put up with aguentar

Q

quality qualidade f; **of good/poor quality** de boa/má qualidade
quarter quarto m; **a quarter of an hour** um quarto de hora; **a quarter to ten** um quarto para as dez, dez menos um quarto
quay cais m
question (n) pergunta f
queue (n) fila f
queue (v) fazer fila
quick rápido m/rápida f
quickly rapidamente
quiet (silent) silencioso m/silenciosa f; (peaceful) tranquilo m/tranquila f
quite bastante; **quite a lot of money** bastante dinheiro; **quite a lot of things** bastantes coisas

R

racist racista mf
racket (tennis, badminton) raquete f
radiator radiador m
radio rádio m
radio station estação f de rádio
rain (n) chuva f
rain (v) chover; **it's raining** está a chover
raincoat gabardine f
random: at random ao acaso
rape (v) violar
rare (infrequent) raro m/rara f; (meat) mal passado m/mal passada f
rarely raramente
rash irritação f de pele, brotoeja f
rather (quite) bastante; **I'd rather have some juice** prefiro um sumo
raw cru m/crua f
razor gilete f; (electric) máquina f de barbear

razor blade lâmina f de barbear
reach (get to) chegar a
read ler
ready pronto m/pronta f
reasonable razoável
receipt recibo m **85**, **110**
receive receber
reception recepção f **41**
receptionist recepcionista mf
recipe receita f
recognize reconhecer
recommend recomendar
red (in colour) vermelho m/vermelha f; (hair) ruivo m/ruiva f
red light semáforo m vermelho
reduce reduzir
reduction redução f
refrigerator frigorífico m
refund (n) reembolso m; **to get a refund** ser reembolsado m/reembolsada f **88**
refund (v) reembolsar
refuse (v) recusar
registered registado m/registada f
registration number (car) matrícula f do carro
remember lembrar-se (de)
remind lembrar
remove remover
rent (n) (house) renda f; (of bike, car) aluguer m
rent (v) (house) arrendar; (bike, car) alugar **42**
rental aluguer m
reopen reabrir
repair reparação f; **to get something repaired** mandar reparar alguma coisa
repeat repetir
reserve reservar
reserved reservado m/reservada f
rest: the rest o resto
rest (v) descansar
restaurant restaurante m
return (n) regresso m
return ticket bilhete m de ida e volta
reverse-charge call chamada f a cobrar no destino **102**

reverse gear marcha-atrás f
rheumatism reumatismo m
rib costela f
right (n) direito m; **to have the right to ...** ter o direito de ...; **to the right (of)** à direita (de)
right (adj) direito m/direita f
right: right away imediatamente; **right beside** mesmo ao lado
ring (n) anel m
ripe maduro m/madura f
rip-off roubo m
risk (n) risco m
river rio m
road estrada f
road sign sinal m de trânsito
rock rocha f
rollerblades patins mpl em linha
room quarto m **38**, **39**
round (adj) redondo m/redonda f
roundabout rotunda f
rubbish lixo m; **to take the rubbish out** pôr o lixo na rua
rucksack mochila f
rug tapete m
ruins ruínas fpl; **in ruins** em ruínas
run (v) correr; (of bus, train) circular; (of machine, car) funcionar
run out of (petrol, money) ficar sem

S

sad triste
safe (adj) seguro m/segura f
safe deposit box cofre m
safety segurança f
safety belt cinto m de segurança
sail velejar; (depart) zarpar
sailing vela f; **to go sailing** fazer vela
sale: for sale vende-se
sales saldos mpl
salt sal m
salty salgado m/salgada f
same igual; **(I'll have) the same** (quero) o mesmo/a mesma
sand areia f

sandals sandálias fpl
sanitary towel penso m higiénico
Saturday sábado m
saucepan tacho m
save (rescue) salvar; (money) poupar; (computer file) guardar
say dizer; **how do you say ... ?** como se diz ...?
scared: to be scared (of) ter medo (de)
scarf (wool) cachecol m; (silk) écharpe f
scenery paisagem f
scissors tesoura f
scoop (of ice cream) bola f
scooter Vespa® f, lambreta f
Scotland Escócia f
Scottish escocês m/escocesa f
scuba diving mergulho m; **to go scuba diving** fazer mergulho
sculpture escultura f
sea mar m
seafood marisco m
seasick: to be seasick sentir-se enjoado m/enjoada f
seaside: at the seaside na praia
seaside resort estância f balnear
season (n) estação f do ano
seat lugar m **24**; (of car, bike) assento m
seatbelt cinto m de segurança
sea view vista f para o mar
seaweed algas fpl
second segundo m/segunda f
secondary school escola f secundária
second class segunda classe f
second-hand em segunda mão
secure (adj) seguro m/segura f
security segurança f
see ver; **see you later!** até mais tarde!; **see you soon!** até breve!; **see you tomorrow!** até amanhã!
seem parecer; **it seems that ...** parece que ...
seldom raras vezes
self-catering com cozinha
sell vender
Sellotape® fita-cola f
send enviar

sender remetente *mf*
sense *(n)* sentido *m*
sensitive sensível
sentence frase *f*
separate *(adj)* separado *m*/separada *f*
separately separadamente
September Setembro *m*
serious *(person)* sério *m*/séria *f*; *(accident, illness)* grave
service serviço *m* **50**
several vários *mpl*/várias *fpl*
sex sexo *m*
shade sombra *f*; **in the shade** à sombra
shame vergonha *f*
shampoo champô *m*
shape forma *f*
share *(v)* partilhar
shave *(legs)* rapar; *(beard)* barbear-se
shaving cream creme *m* de barbear
shaving foam espuma *f* de barbear
she ela
sheet *(for bed)* lençol *m*
shirt camisa *f*
shock choque *m*
shocking chocante
shoes sapatos *mpl*
shop *(n)* loja *f*
shop assistant vendedor *m*/vendedora *f*
shopkeeper comerciante *mf*
shopping compras *fpl*; **to do some/the shopping** fazer algumas/as compras
shopping centre centro *m* comercial
short *(hair, clothes)* curto *m*/curta *f*; *(person)* baixo *m*/baixa *f*; **I'm two euros short** faltam-me dois euros
short cut atalho *m*
shorts calções *mpl*
short-sleeved de manga curta
shoulder ombro *m*
show *(n)* espectáculo *m*
show *(v)* mostrar; *(movie)* passar
shower chuveiro *m*; **to take a shower** tomar um banho de chuveiro
shower gel gel *m* de banho
shut *(v)* fechar
shuttle bus autocarro *m* de ligação,

navete *f*
shy tímido *m*/tímida *f*
sick: to feel sick sentir-se mal
side lado *m*
sign sinal *m*
signal sinal *m*
signature assinatura *f*
silent silencioso *m*/silenciosa *f*
silver prata *f*
silver-plated prateado *m*/prateada *f*
since desde
sing cantar
singer cantor *m*/cantora *f*
single *(person)* solteiro *m*/solteira *f*
single (ticket) bilhete *m* só de ida
sister irmã *f*
sit down sentar-se
size tamanho *m*
ski *(v)* esquiar
ski boots botas *fpl* de esqui
skiing esqui *m*; **to go skiing** fazer esqui, esquiar
ski lift teleférico *m*
ski pole bastão *m* de esqui
ski resort estância *f* de esqui
skin pele *f*
skirt saia *f*
sky céu *m*
skyscraper arranha-céus *m*
sleep *(n)* sono *m*
sleep *(v)* dormir; **to sleep with** dormir com
sleeping bag saco-cama *m*
sleeping pill comprimido *m* para dormir
sleepy: to be sleepy ter sono
sleeve manga *f*
slice fatia *f*
sliced em fatias
slow lento *m*/lenta *f*
slowly lentamente
small pequeno *m*/pequena *f*
smell *(n)* cheiro *m*
smell *(v)* cheirar; **to smell good/bad** cheirar bem/mal
smile *(n)* sorriso *m*
smile *(v)* sorrir

smoke (n) fumo m
smoke (v) fumar
smoker fumador m/fumadora f
snack lanche m
snorkel respirador m, tubo m de respiração
snow (n) neve f
snow (v) nevar
snowboarding (fazer) snowboard
so (very) tão; **so expensive** tão caro; **so that** para; **so much** tanto; **so many** tantos/tantas
soap sabonete m
soccer futebol m
socks meias fpl
some algum m/alguma f; **some people** algumas pessoas
somebody, someone alguém
something alguma coisa; **something else** outra coisa
sometimes às vezes, por vezes
somewhere algures; **somewhere else** noutro lugar
son filho m
song canção f
soon (in a short time) em breve; (early) cedo; **as soon as** assim que; **it's too soon** é demasiado cedo
sore: to have a sore throat ter dor de garganta; **to have a sore head** ter dor de cabeça
sorry! desculpe!
south sul m; **in the south** no sul; **(to the) south of** a sul de
souvenir lembrança f
Spain Espanha f
Spanish espanhol m/espanhola f; (language) espanhol m
spare (adj) (not in use) disponível; (as reserve) a mais
spare part peça f sobresselente
spare tyre pneu m sobresselente
spare wheel roda f sobresselente
spark plug vela f
speak falar **7, 9, 103, 114**
special especial; **today's special** prato m do dia

speciality especialidade f
speed velocidade f; **at full speed** a toda a velocidade
spell soletrar; **how do you spell it?** como se escreve?
spend (money) gastar; (time, holiday) passar
spider aranha f
splinter lasca f
split up separar-se
spoil estragar
sponge esponja f
spoon colher f
sport desporto m
sports ground campo m de jogos
sporty desportivo m/desportiva f
spot (place) local m; (on skin) borbulha f
sprain: to sprain one's ankle torcer o pé
spring Primavera f
square (n) (place) praça f; (shape) quadrado m
square (adj) quadrado m/quadrada f
stadium estádio m
stain mancha f
stained-glass windows vitrais mpl
stairs escadas fpl
stamp (n) selo m **96**
start (v) começar
state (n) estado m
statement declaração f
station estação f
statue estátua f
stay (n) estadia f
stay (v) ficar; **to stay in touch** manter-se em contacto
steal roubar **114, 115**
step (n) degrau m
sticking plaster adesivo m
still (adj) (motionless) imóvel; (not fizzy) sem gás
sting (n) picada f
sting (v) picar; **to get stung (by)** ser picado m/picada f (por) **109**
stock: out of stock esgotado m/esgotada f

stomach estômago m
stone (rock) pedra f; (in fruit) caroço m
stop (v) parar
stopcock válvula f
storey andar m
storm tempestade f
straight ahead, straight on sempre em frente
strange estranho m/estranha f
street rua f
strong forte
stuck preso m/presa f
student estudante mf **23**, **73**
studies estudos mpl
study estudar
style estilo m
subtitled legendado m/legendada f
suffer sofrer
suggest sugerir
suit (n) fato m
suit: does that suit you? está bem?
suitcase mala f
summer Verão m
summit (of mountain) cume m
sun sol m; **in the sun** ao sol
sunbathe tomar banhos de sol
sunburnt: to get sunburnt queimar-se (com o sol)
sun cream protector m solar
Sunday domingo m
sunglasses óculos mpl de sol
sunhat chapéu m (de sol)
sunrise nascer-do-sol m
sunset pôr-do-sol m
sunstroke insolação f; **to get sunstroke** apanhar uma insolação
supermarket supermercado m **42**, **83**
supplement suplemento m
sure seguro m/segura f
surf fazer surf
surfboard prancha f de surf
surfing surf m; **to go surfing** fazer surf
surgical spirit álcool m etílico
surname sobrenome m, nome m de família
surprise (n) surpresa f

surprise (v) fazer uma surpresa a; (astonish) surpreender
sweat (n) suor m
sweat (v) suar
sweater camisola f (de algodão)
sweet (n) doce m; (candy) rebuçado m
sweet (adj) doce
swim: to go for a swim ir nadar
swim (v) nadar
swimming natação f
swimming pool piscina f **80**
swimming trunks calções-de-banho mpl
swimsuit fato-de-banho m
switchboard operator telefonista mf
switch off desligar
switch on ligar
swollen inchado m/inchada f
synagogue sinagoga f
syrup (medicine) xarope m

T

table mesa f **46**, **47**
tablespoon colher f de servir
tablet comprimido m
take levar; (taxi, train) apanhar; **it takes two hours** demora duas horas; **to take a photo** tirar uma fotografia
takeaway (place) restaurante m de comida para levar
take off (plane) descolar, levantar voo
talk falar
tall alto m/alta f
tampon tampão m
tan (n) bronzeado m
tanned bronzeado m/bronzeada f
tap torneira f
taste (n) sabor m
taste (v) provar
tax taxa f
tax-free tax-free
taxi táxi m **33**
taxi driver taxista mf
T-bar telesqui m
team equipa f
teaspoon colher f de chá

teenager adolescente *mf*
telephone (*n*) telefone *m*
telephone (*v*) telefonar
television televisão *f*
tell dizer
temperature temperatura *f*; **to have a temperature** ter febre
temporary temporário *m*/temporária *f*
tennis ténis *m*
tennis court campo *m* de ténis
tennis shoes sapatilhas *fpl* de ténis
tent tenda *f*
tent peg estaca *f*
terminal (*at airport*) terminal *m*
terrace terraço *m*
terrible terrível
thank agradecer; **thank you** obrigado *m*/obrigada *f*; **thank you very much** muito obrigado/obrigada
thanks obrigado *m*/obrigada *f*; **thanks to** graças a
that que; **that one** aquele *m*/aquela *f*
the (*singular*) o *m*/a *f*; (*plural*) os *mpl*/as *fpl* (*see grammar*)
theatre teatro *m*
theft roubo *m*
their deles *mpl*/delas *fpl*; **their car** o carro deles/delas; **their friends** os amigos deles/delas
theirs deles *mpl*/delas *fpl*; **a friend of theirs** um amigo deles/delas; **it's theirs** é deles/delas; **theirs are here** os/as deles/delas estão aqui
them (*direct object*) os *mpl*/as *fpl*; (*indirect object*) lhes; (*after preposition*) eles *mpl*/elas *fpl*; **I know them** eu conheço-os/eu conheço-as; **I don't know them** não os/as conheço; **I asked them** pergunteilhes; **for them** para eles/elas
theme park parque *m* de atracções
themselves (*reflexive*) se; (*after preposition*) eles/elas; **they hurt themselves** eles/elas magoaram-se; **they didn't hurt themselves** eles/elas não se magoaram
then (*afterwards*) depois

there ali; **there is no space** não há espaço; **there are too many people** há demasiada gente; **there is a man outside** está um homem lá fora; **there you are** aqui tem
therefore por conseguinte
thermometer termómetro *m*
Thermos® flask termo *m*
these estes *mpl*/estas *fpl*; **these ones** estes/estas
they eles *mpl*/elas *fpl*; **they say that …** dizem que …
thief ladrão *m*/ladra *f*
thigh coxa *f*
thin magro *m*/magra *f*
thing coisa *f*; **things** as coisas; **where are my things?** onde estão as minhas coisas?
think pensar
think about pensar (em)
thirsty: to be thirsty ter sede
this este *m*/esta *f*; **this one** este/esta; **this evening** esta noite; **this is** este/esta/isto é
those esses *mpl*/essas *fpl*; **those ones** esses/essas
thread linha *f*
throat garganta *f*
throw atirar
throw out jogar fora
Thursday quinta-feira *f*
ticket bilhete *m* **23**, **66**, **67**
ticket office bilheteira *f*
tidy arrumado *m*/arrumada *f*
tie gravata *f*
tight apertado *m*/apertada *f*
tights collants *mpl*
time tempo *m*; (*on clock*) horas *fpl* **122**; (*occasion*) vez *f*; **what time is it?** que horas são?; **from time to time** de vez em quando; **on time** a horas; **three/four times** três/quatro vezes
time difference diferença *f* horária
timetable horário *m* **23**
tinfoil folha *f* de alumínio
tip (*for waiter*) gorjeta *f*

tired cansado m/cansada f
tissue lenço m de papel
tobacco tabaco m
tobacconist's tabacaria f
today hoje
toe dedo m do pé
together juntos mpl/juntas fpl; **we're together** estamos juntos/juntas; **all together** (everything) tudo junto
toilet casa-de-banho f **7**
toilet bag estojo m de toilette
toilet paper papel-higiénico m
toiletries artigos mpl de toilette
toll portagem f
tomorrow amanhã; **tomorrow evening** amanhã à noite; **tomorrow morning** amanhã de manhã
tongue língua f
tonight hoje à noite
too demasiado m/demasiada f, demais; (also) também; **too bad** é uma pena (que); **too many** demasiados/demasiadas; **too much** demasiado; **me too** eu também
tooth dente m
toothbrush escova f de dentes
toothpaste pasta f de dentes
top (n) (highest point) topo m; **at the top** no topo
torch lanterna f
touch tocar
tour visita f
tour guide guia mf
tourist turista mf
tourist office posto m de turismo
tourist trap armadilha f para turistas
towards na direcção de
towel toalha f
town cidade f; (small) vila f
town centre centro m da cidade
town hall câmara f municipal
toy brinquedo m
traditional tradicional
traffic trânsito m
traffic jam engarrafamento m
traffic lights semáforos mpl

train comboio m **29**; **the train to Porto** o comboio para o Porto
train station estação f de comboios
tram eléctrico m
tram stop paragem m de eléctrico
transfer (n) (of money) transferência f
transfer (v) (money) transferir
translate traduzir
travel agency agência f de viagens
travel viajar
traveller's cheque cheque m de viagem
tray tabuleiro m
trip viagem f; **have a good trip!** boa viagem!
trolley carrinho m
trouble: to have trouble doing something ter problemas a fazer alguma coisa
trousers calças fpl
true verdadeiro m/verdadeira f
try (attempt) tentar; (food) provar; **to try to do something** tentar fazer alguma coisa
try on experimentar
Tuesday terça-feira f
tube (train) metro m
tube station estação f do metro
turn (n) (go) vez f; **it's your turn** é a sua vez
turn (v) virar
twice duas vezes
type (n) tipo m
type (v) escrever
typical típico m/típica f
tyre pneu m

U

ugly feio m/feia f
umbrella guarda-chuva m
uncle tio m
uncomfortable desconfortável
under (beneath) debaixo (de)
underground (n) metro m
underground line linha f do metro
underground station estação f do metro

underneath debaixo (de)
understand compreender **9**
underwear roupa *f* interior
United Kingdom Reino *m* Unido
United States Estados *mpl* Unidos
until até
upset transtornado *m*/transtornada *f*
upstairs andar de cima; **I live upstairs** moro no andar de cima; **to go/come upstairs** subir; **the upstairs windows** as janelas do andar de cima
urgent urgente
us nos; *(after preposition)* nós; **he knows us** ele conhece-nos; **she didn't ask us** ela não nos perguntou; **for us** para nós; **with us** connosco *(see grammar)*
use *(v)* utilizar, usar; **to be used for** ser para; **I'm used to it** estou habituado *m*/habituada *f*
useful útil
useless inútil
usually habitualmente
U-turn meia-volta *f*

V

vaccinated (against) vacinado *m*/vacinada *f* (contra)
valid válido *m*/válida *f*
valley vale *m*
VAT IVA *m*
vegetarian vegetariano *m*/vegetariana *f*
very muito
view vista *f*
villa vivenda *f*
village aldeia *f*
visa visto *m*
visit *(n)* visita *f*
visit *(v)* visitar
volleyball voleibol *m*
vomit *(v)* vomitar

W

waist cintura *f*
wait esperar; **to wait for somebody/ something** esperar alguém/alguma coisa
waiter empregado *m* de mesa
waitress empregada *f* de mesa
wake up acordar, despertar
Wales País *m* de Gales
walk: to go for a walk dar um passeio
walk *(v)* caminhar; *(leisurely)* passear; **we get there faster if we walk** chegamos lá mais depressa se formos a pé
walking: to go walking caminhar
walking boots botas *fpl* de caminhar
Walkman® Walkman® *m*
wallet carteira *f* (de documentos)
want querer; **to want to do something** querer fazer alguma coisa
warm quente
warn avisar
wash: to have a wash lavar-se
wash *(v)* lavar; **to wash one's hair** lavar a cabeça
washbasin pia *f*
washing: to do the washing lavar roupa
washing machine máquina *f* de lavar roupa
washing powder detergente *m* para a roupa
washing-up liquid detergente *m* para a louça
wasp vespa *f*
waste *(n)* desperdício *m*
watch *(n)* relógio *m* (de pulso)
watch *(v)* *(observe)* ver; *(look after)* tomar conta (de); **watch out!** cuidado!
water água *f*
water heater aquecedor *m* da água
waterproof à prova de água
waterskiing esqui *m* aquático
wave *(in sea)* onda *f*
way *(route)* caminho *m*; *(direction)* direcção *f*; *(manner)* maneira *f*; **this way, please** por aqui, se faz favor
way in entrada *f*
way out saída *f*
we nós
weak fraco *m*/fraca *f*

wear *(clothes)* vestir; *(shoes)* calçar; *(glasses, perfume)* usar
weather tempo *m*; **the weather's bad** o tempo está mau
weather forecast previsão *f* do tempo **20**
website sítio *m* da Web
Wednesday quarta-feira *f*
week semana *f*
weekend fim-de-semana *m*
welcome bem-vindo *m*/bem-vinda *f*; **welcome!** bem-vindos!; **you're welcome** de nada!
well bem; **I'm very well** estou bem; **well done** *(meat)* bem-passado *m*/bem-passada *f*
Welsh galês *m*/galesa *m*; *(language)* galês *m*
west oeste *m*; **in the west** no oeste; **(to the) west of** a oeste de
wet molhado *m*/molhada *f*
wetsuit fato *m* de mergulho
what o que; **what do you want?** o que deseja?
wheel *(of car, bike)* roda *f*; *(steering wheel)* volante *m*
wheelchair cadeira *f* de rodas
when quando
where onde; **where is/are …?** onde é/são …?; **where are you from?** de onde é?; **where are you going?** para onde vão?
which qual, que
while enquanto; **while he ate** enquanto ele comia; **while travelling** durante a viagem; **wait a while** esperar um momento
white branco *m*/branca *f*
who quem; **who's calling?** quem fala?
whole todo *m*/toda *f*; **the whole cake** o bolo todo
whose *(one)* cujo *m*/cuja *f*; *(more than one)* cujos *mpl*/cujas *fpl*; **whose …?** de quem …?
why porque; **why?** porquê?
wide largo *m*/larga *f*
wife esposa *f*
wild selvagem

wind vento *m*
window janela *f*; **in the window** à janela
windscreen pára-brisas *m*
windsurfing windsurf *m*; **to go windsurfing** fazer windsurf
winter Inverno *m*
with com
withdraw *(money)* levantar
without sem
woman mulher *f*
wood madeira *f*
wool lã *f*
work *(n)* trabalho *m*; **work of art** obra *f* de arte
work *(v)* trabalhar **14**
works obras *fpl*
world mundo *m*
worse pior; **to get worse** piorar; **it's worse (than)** é pior (do que)
worth: to be worth valer a pena; **it's worth it** vale a pena
wound *(n)* ferida *f*
wrist pulso *m*
write escrever **10**
wrong errado *m*/errada *f*

XYZ

X-ray radiografia *f*

year ano *m*
yellow amarelo *m*/amarela *f*
yes sim
yesterday ontem; **yesterday evening** ontem à noite
you *see grammar*
young jovem
your *see grammar*
yours *see grammar*
yourself *see grammar*
yourselves *see grammar*
youth hostel pousada *f* da juventude

zero zero *m*
zip fecho *m*
zoo jardim *m* zoológico
zoom (lens) zoom *m*

DICTIONARY

PORTUGUESE-ENGLISH

A

a (prep) to; (time) at; **à esquerda** on the left; **à janela** by the window; **à meia-noite** at midnight; **a dez milhas (daqui)** 10 miles away; **ir ao cinema/a Lisboa** go to the cinema/to Lisbon

a(s) (art) the

a(s) (pron) it; you; her; them; **eu conheço-a(s)** I know you/her/them; **não a encontro** I can't find it (see grammar)

abadia abbey

abaixo down; **rua/escadas abaixo** down the street/stairs; **abaixo de** below

abelha bee

aberto/a open

abre-latas can opener

Abril April

abrir to open

acabar to finish

acampar to go camping; to camp

acaso: por acaso by chance; **ao acaso** at random

aceitar to accept

acender (candle, cigarette) to light; (light, TV) to turn on

achar to find

acidente accident

acima up; **acima de** above; **acima de tudo** above all; **escadas/rua acima** up the stairs/street

acompanhar to accompany

aconselhar to advise

acontecer to happen

acordar to wake up

acreditar to believe

adaptador adaptor

adesivo sticking plaster

adeus goodbye

adiantado (adv) in advance

adoecer to fall ill

adolescente teenager

adorar to love

adulto/a adult

advogado/a lawyer

aeroporto airport

afogar-se to drown

agência de viagens travel agency

agora now

Agosto August

agradar: agradar a to please; **não me agrada** I don't like it

agradável pleasant

agradecer to thank

água water

água potável drinking water

agulha needle

ainda still; yet; **ainda falta um** one is still missing; **ainda não** not yet; **ainda bem** just as well

ajuda help

ajudar to help

álcool alcohol

aldeia village

alérgico/a allergic

alfândega customs

algas seaweed

algodão cotton

alguém somebody, someone

algum(a) some; **alguma coisa** something

alguns/algumas some; **algumas pessoas** some people

ali (over) there; **é por ali** it's that way

almoçar to have lunch
almoço lunch
almofada pillow
alojamento accommodation
alojar to put someone up
alto/a high; tall; *(noise)* loud
alugar to rent, to hire; **alugar a** to rent out to
aluguer rent
amanhã tomorrow; **amanhã de manhã/à noite** tomorrow morning/evening
amarelo/a yellow
amargo/a bitter
ambos/as both
ambulância ambulance
americano/a American
amigo/a friend
amor love
anca hip
andar *(n)* floor
andar *(v)* to walk
andar de bicicleta to cycle
andebol handball
anel ring
anestesia anaesthetic
animado/a lively
animal animal
aniversário anniversary; birthday; **feliz aniversário** happy birthday
ano year; **Ano Novo** New Year
anterior previous
antes (de) before
antibiótico antibiotic
anticoncepcional contraceptive
antigo/a old; ancient
apagar to delete; *(light)* to put out
apanhar *(illness, ball)* to catch; *(flowers, fruit)* to pick; *(fallen object)* to pick up
aparelhagem hi-fi
apartamento flat
apenas only, just; **apenas um** just one
apendicite appendicitis
apertado/a tight
apoiar to support; **apoiar em** to rest against

apontar para to point at
aprender to learn
apresentar to present; **apresentar alguém a alguém** to introduce someone to someone
aproveitar-se de to take advantage of
aquecedor heater; **aquecedor eléctrico/a gás** electric/gas heater
aquecedor da água water heater
aquecimento heating
aquele/a that; that one
aqui here; **aqui está/estão** here is/are; **até aqui** up to now; **por aqui, se faz favor** this way, please
aquilo that
ar air; **ao ar livre** in the open air
ar-condicionado air conditioning
aranha spider
área area
areia sand
arranha-céus skyscraper
arrendar to rent
arrumado/a tidy
arte art
artesanato handicraft
artigo article
artista artist
árvore tree
Ásia Asia
asma asthma
aspirina aspirin
assalto robbery
assim like this; **assim assim** so-so; **assim que** as soon as
assinar to sign
assinatura signature
atacar to attack
atalho short cut
ataque attack
ataque cardíaco heart attack
até *(time)* until; *(distance)* as far as; *(height, quantity)* up to; **até amanhã** see you tomorrow; **até ao pescoço/aos pés** up to the neck/down to the feet
atenção attention; **atenção!** look out!
atestar to fill up

atirar to throw; *(with gun)* to shoot; **atirar ao chão** to knock over; **atirar fora** to throw away
atrás (de) behind
atrasado/a delayed; late
atraso delay
através through; by way of
atravessar to cross
atrevido/a forward
atropelado/a: ser atropelado/a to be run over
aula lesson
autocarro bus; coach
auto-estrada motorway
automóvel car; **de automóvel** by car
autor(a) author
avaria breakdown
avariar to break down
ave bird
avenida avenue
avião aeroplane; **por avião** by air/airmail
avisar to warn
aviso notice; warning
azul blue

B

bagagem luggage; **bagagem de mão** hand luggage
bairro area; neighbourhood
baixa *(n)* city centre
baixo *(adv) (speak, laugh)* quietly; **no andar de baixo** downstairs; **em/por baixo de** under(neath)
baixo/a *(adj)* low; short
balão balloon
balcão counter
banco stool; seat; *(for money)* bank; *(in hospital)* casualty; **banco de jardim** bench
bandeira flag
banheira bathtub
banho bath; **tomar banho** to have a bath/a shower; *(in sea, river)* to have a swim
bar bar

barata *(n)* cockroach
barato/a cheap
barba beard; **fazer a barba** to shave
barbear-se to shave
barco boat
barriga belly; **barriga da perna** calf
barro clay; mud; **de barro** earthenware
barulhento/a noisy
barulho noise
basquete(bol) basketball
bastante a lot, plenty; **bastante dinheiro** a lot of money
bastar to be enough; **basta!** that's enough!
bateria battery
bebé baby
bêbedo/a drunk
beber to drink; **beber um copo** to have a drink
bebida drink
beijar to kiss
beijo kiss
beira-mar seaside; **à beira-mar** by the sea
belo/a beautiful
bem well; **está bem!** OK!, alright!; **tudo bem?** alright?; **estou bem** I'm fine
bem-vindo/a welcome
biberão baby's bottle
biblioteca library
bicha queue; **fazer bicha** to queue
bicicleta bike
bigode moustache
bilhete ticket; **bilhete só de ida** single (ticket); **bilhete de ida e volta** return (ticket)
bilhete de identidade identity card
bilheteira ticket office
binóculos binoculars
biológico/a organic
boa see **bom**
boas-vindas welcome
boca mouth
bóia buoy
bola ball
boleia: pedir/viajar à boleia to hitch-hike

bolha (de água) blister
bolso pocket
bom/boa good; **bom dia** good morning; **boa tarde** good afternoon; **boa noite** good evening
bomba de bicicleta bicycle pump
bombas (de gasolina) petrol station
bombeiros fire brigade
boné cap
bonito/a pretty
borbulha spot *(on skin)*
bosque woods
botas boots
botão button
botija de gás gas cylinder
braço arm
branco/a white
breve brief; **em breve** soon; **até breve** see you soon
briga fight
brincar to play
brincos earrings
brinquedo toy
brochura brochure
bronquite bronchitis
bronzeado *(n)* tan
bronzeado/a tanned
bronzear-se to get a tan
buraco hole
buscar to look for; **ir buscar alguma coisa** to fetch something; **ir buscar alguém** to pick somebody up

C

cabeça head
cabeleireiro/a hairdresser
cabelo hair
cabide coathanger
cabine (telefónica) phone box
cabine de provas changing room
cabra goat
cacete stick; *(bread)* baguette
cachecol scarf
cacifo locker

cada each; **cada um(a)** each one; **cada dois dias** every other day
cadeira chair
cadeira de rodas wheelchair
caderno notebook
café *(drink)* coffee; *(place)* café
caiaque kayak
cair to fall
cais (de embarque) quay
caixa box; *(in supermarket, shop)* checkout; *(in bank)* cashier
caixa automático cashpoint
caixa de velocidades gearbox
caixa do correio letterbox
caixote box
caixote do lixo bin
calçar to put on
calças trousers
calças de ganga jeans
calções shorts
calções-de-banho swimming trunks
calmo/a calm; quiet
calor heat; **estar com calor** to feel hot; **está calor** it's hot
cama bed
camada layer
câmara (fotográfica) camera
câmara de vídeo camcorder
câmara municipal town hall
câmbio exchange rate
camião lorry
caminhar to walk
caminho way; path; **a/no caminho** on the way
camisa shirt; **camisa de noite** nightdress
camisola jumper
campismo camping; **fazer campismo** to go camping
campista camper
campo countryside
campo de futebol football pitch
campo de golfe golf course
campo de ténis tennis court
canal channel; canal
canção song
cancelar to cancel

candeeiro lamp
caneta pen
cano pipe
canoagem canoeing; **fazer canoagem** to go canoeing
cansaço tiredness
cansado/a tired
cansativo/a tiring
cantar to sing
cantil water bottle; flask
cantor(a) singer
cão dog
capacete helmet
capela chapel
cara face
caravana caravan
cárie: ter uma cárie to have a bad tooth
caro/a expensive
caroço (in fruit) stone
carregar to carry: **carregar em** to press
carrinho trolley
carrinho de bebé pram, pushchair
carro car; **de carro** by car
carruagem coach, carriage
carta letter; (playing) card; **carta registada** recorded letter
carta de condução driving licence
cartão card
cartão de crédito credit card
cartão de débito debit card
cartão telefónico phonecard
cartaz poster
carteira wallet; handbag
carteiro postman
carteirista pickpocket
casa house; **em casa** at home; **ir para casa** to go home
casa-de-banho bathroom; toilet
casa de câmbio bureau de change
casaco jacket; cardigan
casado/a married
casamento wedding
caso: em caso de in case of
cassete cassette, tape
castanho/a brown
castelo castle

catedral cathedral
católico/a catholic
causa cause; **por causa de** because of
cavalo horse
cedo soon; early; **é demasiado cedo** it's too soon
cego/a blind
cemitério cemetery
centímetro centimetre
centro centre
centro comercial shopping centre
centro da cidade town centre
centro de saúde clinic
cerca: cerca de about, around
certo/a correct; certain
céu sky
chá tea
chamada call; **chamada a cobrar no destino** reverse-charge call; **chamada local** local call
chamar to call; **chamar-se** to be called
champô shampoo
chão floor; ground; **no chão** on the floor
chapéu hat; umbrella
chapéu de chuva umbrella
chapéu de praia beach umbrella
charuto cigar
chave key
chávena cup
chefe boss
chegada arrival
chegar to arrive; to be enough; **já chega!** that's enough!
cheio/a full
cheirar to smell; **to smell good/bad** cheirar bem/mal
cheiro smell
cheque cheque
cheque de viagem traveller's cheque
chichi: fazer chichi to pee
chinelos (de quarto) slippers
chinelos de dedo flip-flops
chocante shocking
chocolate chocolate
choque shock; crash
chorar to cry

chover to rain; **está a chover** it's raining
chumbo lead; *(in tooth)* filling; **sem chumbo** unleaded
chupeta dummy
churrasco barbecue
chuva rain
chuveiro shower
ciber-café Internet café
cidade city
cigarro cigarette
cima: de cima above; **de cima de** off; **em cima de** on; on top of; **por cima de** over; **parte de cima** upper part
cinema cinema
cinto belt
cinto de segurança seatbelt
cintura waist
cinzeiro ashtray
cinzento/a grey
circo circus
circulação circulation
claro/a *(adj)* light; *(sky)* clear; **azul-claro** light blue
claro *(adv)* clear; **é claro!** of course!
classe class
classe económica economy class
classe executiva business class
clima climate
clínico geral GP
clube club; **clube nocturno** nightclub
cobertor blanket
cobrar to charge
cobrir to cover
código code
código pessoal PIN (number)
código postal postcode
coelho rabbit
cofre safe deposit box
coisa thing
cola glue
colar *(n)* necklace
colar *(v)* to glue
colchão mattress
colecção collection
colher spoon
colina hill

collants tights
colónia colony; *(perfume)* cologne
colónia de férias summer camp
com with
comboio train
começar to begin
comer to eat
comerciante shopkeeper
comércio commerce
comida food
comigo with me
comissão commission
como like; as; how; **bem como** as well as; **como está?** how are you?
companhia company
companhia aérea airline
compartimento compartment
completo/a complet
comprar to buy
compras shopping; **fazer as compras** to do the shopping; **ir às compras** to go shopping
compreender to understand
comprido/a long
comprimido *(n)* tablet; **comprimido para as dores** painkiller
computador computer
computador portátil laptop
concerto concert
concha seashell
concordar to agree
condimentado/a spicy
conduzir to drive
confiança trust
confiar: confiar algo a alguém to entrust someone with something; **confiar em alguém** to trust someone
confirmar to confirm
confortável comfortable
congelado/a frozen
congelador freezer
conhecer to know
conhecido/a well-known
conjunto set; *(musical)* band, group
connosco with us

conseguir: conseguir fazer to manage to do
conselho advice
consigo with you; with him; with her; with them
constipação cold (*illness*)
constipado/a: estar constipado/a to have a cold
construído/a built
construir to build
consulado consulate
consulta appointment
conta bill
conta bancária bank account
contactar to contact
contacto contact
contador meter
contador da electricidade electricity meter
contagioso/a contagious
contar to count; **contar com** to count on
contente happy
contigo with you
continuação continuation
continuar to continue
contra against
contraceptivo contraceptive
contrário/a opposite; **na direcção contrária/no sentido contrário** in the opposite direction
contrato contract
convidar to invite
convosco with you
cópia copy
copo glass; **um copo de água** a glass of water
cor colour
coração heart
coragem courage
cordeiro lamb
cor-de-laranja orange
cor-de-rosa pink
corpo body
correcto/a correct
correio mail, post; **pelo correio** by post

correio aéreo airmail
corrente current; chain
correr to run
correspondência correspondence
cortar to cut; **cortar-se** to cut oneself
corta-unhas nail clippers
cortiça cork
costa coast
costas back
costela rib
cotonete cotton bud
couro leather
coxa thigh
cozinha kitchen
cozinhar to cook
creme cream
creme de barbear shaving cream
creme hidratante moisturizer
creme solar sun cream
crer: crer que to believe that
crescer to grow
criança child
crise crisis
cru(a) raw
cruz cross
cruzamento junction; crossroads
cruzeiro cruise
cubo de gelo ice cube
cuecas underpants; knickers
cuidado care; **cuidado!** watch out!; **cuidado com ...** beware of ...; **com cuidado** carefully
cuidar: cuidar de to look after
cujo/a whose
cume summit
curar to cure
curso course
curto/a short
custar to cost

dados details; data
dança dance
dançar to dance
danificado/a damaged

daqui from here; **daqui a um mês** in a month; **daqui em diante** from now on; **daqui a pouco** in a little while

dar to give; **dar problemas** to create problems; **dar para a praia** to look out onto the beach; **dar-se bem com alguém** to get on well with someone

data date

data de nascimento date of birth

data de validade/vencimento expiry date

de of; **de carro** by car; **de preto** in black; **de Lisboa** from Lisbon; **mais lento do que** slower than; **de … a …** from … to …

debaixo (de) under, underneath; **por debaixo de** below

decepcionante disappointing

decidir to decide

declaração statement

declarar to declare

dedo finger

dedo do pé toe

defeito flaw

deficiente disabled

degrau step

deitar *(place)* to put; *(spread)* to lay down; *(smoke, smell)* to give off; **deitar algo no lixo** to put something in the bin; **deitar ao chão** to knock over; **deitar fora** to throw away; to spill over; **deitar no correio** to post; **deitar sangue** to bleed

deitar-se to lie down; to go to bed

deixar to let; to leave

dele/a its; his; her; hers; **a bagagem dele** his luggage; **um amigo dela** a friend of hers (see *grammar*)

deles/as their; theirs; **o carro deles/as** their car; **um amigo deles/as** a friend of theirs (see *grammar*)

demais too; too much; too many; **está quente demais** it's too hot; **tem água demais** there's too much water

demasiado/a too; too many; too much

dentada bite

dente tooth

dentista dentist

dentro inside; **dentro do armário** in the wardrobe; **dentro em pouco/de nada** soon; **dentro de uma hora** in an hour

departamento department

depender (de) to depend (on)

depois then; afterwards; later; **depois de** after; **depois do almoço** after lunch

depósito deposit

depósito de bagagem left-luggage (office)

depressa quickly; **depressa!** hurry up!

desagradável unpleasant

desaparecer to disappear

desastre disaster; accident

descansar to rest

descarregar to unload; *(on computer)* to download

descartável disposable

descascar to peel

descer *(hill)* to go down; *(bus)* to get off; *(price, level)* to fall, to decrease

descobrir to discover; to find out

descolar to take off

desconfortável uncomfortable

desconto discount; concession

desculpa excuse

desculpar-se to excuse oneself; **desculpe …** excuse me …; **desculpe!** sorry!

desde since; **desde que** as long as

desejo desire; wish

desenho drawing

desinfectar to disinfect

desistir to give up

desligar to switch off; *(telephone)* to hang up

desmaiar to faint

desodorizante deodorant

despachar-se to hurry (up)

despertador alarm clock

desportivo/a sporty

desporto sport

destinatário/a addressee

detergente para a louça washing-up liquid

detergente para a roupa washing powder

detestar to hate

devagar slowly

dever (n) duty

dever must; should; to owe; **devem ser cinco horas** it must be 5 o'clock; **deve fazer sol amanhã** it should be sunny tomorrow; **dever algo a alguém** to owe something to someone

devolver to give back; to return

Dezembro December

dia day

diabetes diabetes

diante de in front of, before

diapositivo slide

dicionário dictionary

dieta diet; **estar de dieta** to be on a diet

diferença difference

diferença horária time difference

diferente (de) different (from)

difícil difficult

diminuir to decrease

dinheiro money; **pagar em dinheiro** to pay cash

dinheiro trocado small change

direcção direction; **na direcção de** towards

directo/a direct

direito (n) right; **ter o direito de ...** to have the right to ...

direito/a (adj) right; straight; **à direita** on the right; **à direita (de)** to the right (of); **do lado direito** on the right

disco disk; record

discoteca disco

discutir to discuss

disponível spare; available

disso that; **nada disso** nothing like that

DIU coil

divertido/a funny; enjoyable

divertir-se to enjoy oneself

divorciado/a divorced

dizer to say; to tell; **ele disse que ...** he said that ...; **diz-me uma coisa** tell me something

doce sweet

documentos documents

doença illness

doente (adj) ill

doente (n) patient

doer to hurt

doido/a mad

domingo Sunday

dono/a owner

dor pain; **dor de cabeça** headache; **dor de dentes** toothache

dormir to sleep; **dormir com** to sleep with

doutor(a) doctor

drogas drugs

duche shower

duração duration

durante during

durar to last

duro/a hard; (meat) tough

E

e and

écharpe scarf

edifício building

educado/a polite

ele/a he; she; it; **é ele/a** it's him/her

electricidade electricity

eléctrico (n) tram

eléctrico/a (adj) electric

eles/as they; **são eles/as** it's them

elevador lift

em in; on; at; **em Londres** in London; **no domingo** on Sunday; **no hotel** at the hotel

embaixada embassy

embarcar to board

embarque boarding

embora even though; **ir-se embora** to go away

embraiagem clutch

embriagado/a drunk

embrulhar to wrap; **embrulhar para prenda** to gift-wrap

embrulho parcel
ementa menu
emergência emergency
empregado/a employee; **empregado/a de mesa** waiter/waitress
emprego job
emprestar to lend
empurrar to push
encerramento closing
encher to fill
encomenda order; request
encontrar to find; **encontrar-se** to meet
encontro appointment; **marcar um encontro** to make an appointment; **ter um encontro (com)** to have an appointment (with)
endereço address
endereço de e-mail e-mail address
enfermeiro/a nurse
enfim at last
enganar-se to make a mistake
engarrafamento traffic jam
engraçado/a funny
enquanto while; **enquanto ele comia** while he ate
ensinar to teach
então so; well
entornar to spill
entrada admission; entrance; way in; **Boas Entradas!** Happy New Year!
entrar to come in; to go in
entre among; between
envelope envelope
enviar to send
epiléptico/a epileptic
equipa team
equipamento equipment
errado/a wrong
erro mistake
escadas stairs
escalada climbing; **fazer escalada** to go climbing
escocês/esa Scottish
Escócia Scotland
escola school

escolha choice
escolher to choose
escova brush
escova de dentes toothbrush
escrever to write; to type
escultura sculpture
escuro/a dark; *(sky)* overcast; **azul-escuro** dark blue
esforço effort; **fazer um esforço** to make an effort
esgotado/a sold out
especial special
especialidade speciality
espectáculo show
espelho mirror
espelho retrovisor rearview mirror
esperar to expect; to wait; to hope; **esperar alguém** to wait for someone; **espero que** I hope that
esponja sponge
esposa wife
espuma de barbear shaving foam
esquadra (da polícia) police station
esquecer-se to forget
esquerdo/a left; **à esquerda** on the left; **à esquerda (de)** to the left (of); **do lado esquerdo** on the left
esqui skiing; **fazer esqui** to go skiing
esqui aquático waterskiing
esquiar to ski
esquina corner
esse/a that; **esse livro** that book
esses/as those; those ones
estaca tent peg
estação station
estação de comboios train station
estação de correios post office
estação de rádio radio station
estação do ano season
estação do metro tube station
estação rodoviária bus station
estacionamento parking
estacionar to park
estadia stay
estádio stadium
estado state

Estados Unidos United States
estágio traineeship
estância balnear seaside resort
estância de esqui ski resort
estar to be; **está?** hello?; **está frio** it's cold; **como estão?** how are you?
estátua statue
este *(n)* east; **a este de** (to the) east of; **no este** in the east
este/a this; this one; **esta noite** this evening
estes/as these; these ones
estilo style
estojo de toilette toilet bag
estômago stomach
estrada road
estragar to spoil
estrangeiro/a *(adj)* foreign
estrangeiro/a *(n)* foreigner; **no estrangeiro** abroad
estranho/a strange
estudante student
estudar to study
estudos studies
eu I; me; **eu sou inglês** I'm English; **sou eu** it's me
euro euro
Europa Europe
europeu/eia European
excelente excellent
excepcional exceptional
excepto except
excesso excess; **excesso de peso** overweight; **excesso de bagagem** excess luggage
excursão excursion
exemplo example; **por exemplo** for example
êxito success
experimentar to try; to try on
explicar to explain
exposição exhibition
expressão expression
expresso/a express; **por correio expresso** by express post
exterior outside

extra extra
extraordinário/a extraordinary

---

faca knife
face face
fácil easy
facto fact; **de facto** in fact
factura invoice; bill
faixa lane
faixa dos autocarros bus lane
faixa para ciclistas cycle lane
falar to speak; to talk
falésia cliff
falhar to miss
falso/a false; fake
faltar to miss; **faltam duas pessoas** there are two people missing
família family
farmácia chemist's
farmácia de serviço duty chemist's
farol lighthouse
farol dianteiro headlight
farto: estar farto de to be fed up with
fatia slice
fato suit
fato de banho swimsuit
fato de mergulho wetsuit
favor favour; **fazer um favor a alguém** to do someone a favour; **se faz favor** please
favorito/a favourite
fax fax
fazer to make; to do
fazer fila to queue
febre fever; **ter febre** to have a fever
febre dos fenos hay fever
fechado/a closed
fechadura lock
fechar to shut; to close
fechar à chave to lock
fecho zip
feio/a ugly
feira fair; market
feira popular funfair

feliz happy
feriado public holiday
feriado nacional national holiday
férias holiday(s); **de férias** on holiday
ferida *(n)* wound
ferido/a *(adj)* injured
ferro de passar iron
ferver to boil
festa party; festival
festejar to celebrate
Fevereiro February
ficar to stay; to be; **fica-lhe bem** it suits you
ficheiro file
fígado liver
fila queue
filha daughter
filho son
filme film, movie
fim end; **no fim de** at the end of
fim-de-semana weekend
fino/a fine; thin
fio cable
fita-cola Sellotape®
flor flower
floresta forest
fogão stove
fogão de campismo camping stove
fogo fire
fogo de artifício fireworks
folha leaf; **folha de papel** sheet of paper
folha de alumínio tinfoil
folheto leaflet
fome hunger; **ter fome** to be hungry
fora out; **jantar/almoçar fora** to eat out; **estar fora** to be away; **fora de horas** outside working hours; **fora!** get out!; **fora de serviço** out of order
forma shape
formiga ant
formulário form
forno oven
forte strong
fósforo match
fotocópia photocopy
fotografia photo; **tirar uma fotografia (de)** to take a photo (of)

fraco/a weak
fractura fracture
frágil fragile
fralda nappy
frasco jar; bottle
frase sentence
frente front; **em/à frente de** in front of; **para a frente** forward; **sempre em frente** straight ahead
fresco/a cool
frigorífico fridge
frio/a cold; chilly; **está frio** it's cold; **tenho frio** I'm cold
fronha pillowcase
fronteira border
fruta fruit
fuga leak
fumador(a) smoker; **não fumadores** non smoking
fumar to smoke
funcionar to work, to function
fundo *(n)* bottom; **no fundo (de)** at the bottom (of)
fundo/a *(adj)* deep
furado/a pierced; punctured; **ter um pneu furado** to have a flat tyre
furar to pierce; to puncture
furo puncture
fusível fuse
futebol football

G

gabardine raincoat
gaivota seagull
gajo guy
galeria de arte gallery
galês/esa Welsh
galinha chicken
galo cockerel
ganhar to win; to earn
garagem garage
garantia guarantee
garfo fork
garganta throat
garrafa bottle

gás gas
gasóleo diesel
gasolina petrol
gasolina sem chumbo unleaded petrol
gasolina super four-star petrol
gastar *(money)* to spend; *(use up)* to wear out
gato cat
gaze gauze
geada frost
gel de banho shower gel
gelo ice
gémeo/a twin
género type
gente people; **toda a gente** everybody; **muita gente** a lot of people
gentil polite
geral general
gerente manager
gerir to manage
gesso plaster (cast)
gilete disposable razor
ginecologista gynaecologist
golfe golf
gordo/a fat
gorjeta tip
gostar (de) to like; **gostaria de ...** I'd like to ...;
gosto taste; **com gosto** with pleasure
gotas drops
Grã-Bretanha Great Britain
graças a thanks to
gramas grams
grande big
grátis free
grau degree
gravar to record
gravata tie
grave serious
grávida pregnant
gripe flu
gritar to cry
grupo group
guarda policeman
guarda-chuva umbrella
guardanapo napkin

guardar to keep
guarda-sol parasol
guerra war
guia guide

H

hábito habit; **ter o hábito (de)** to be in the habit (of)
haver: há there is/are; **há pessoas que ...** there are people who ...; **há um cinema** there is a cinema; **estive cá há dois anos** I was here two years ago; **vivo aqui há dois anos** I've been living here for two years
hemorróidas piles
hesitar to hesitate
história history
hoje today; **hoje em dia** nowadays; **hoje à noite** tonight
Holanda Holland
holandês/esa Dutch
hóquei hockey; **hóquei em patins** roller hockey
homem man
homossexual homosexual
honesto/a honest
hora hour; **a horas** on time; **a que horas?** at what time?; **hora local** local time
horário timetable
horário de abertura opening time
horário de atendimento opening hours
horário de encerramento closing time
horrível horrible
hóspede guest
hospital hospital
hotel hotel
húmido/a damp

I

ida outward journey
idade age
ideia idea

identificação identity papers
igreja church
igual the same; **para mim é igual** it's all the same to me
ilha island
imóvel still
impermeável waterproof
importância importance; *(money)* amount
importante important
importar-se to mind; **não me importo** I don't mind
impressão impression; **ter a impressão de** to have the impression that
impressionante impressive
imprimir to print
incêndio fire
inchaço bump; swelling
inchado/a swollen
incluído/a included
incomodar to disturb; **não incomodar** do not disturb
incrível incredible
independente independent
indicador indicator
indicativo dialling code
inesquecível unforgettable
infecção infection
informação information
informações directory enquiries
Inglaterra England
inglês/esa English
iniciais initials
início beginning; **no início** at the beginning
injecção injection
inscrever-se to sign up
insecticida insecticide
insecto insect
insolação sunstroke; **apanhar uma insolação** to get sunstroke
insónia insomnia
instrumento instrument
insulto insult
inteiro/a entire; whole
inteligente intelligent

intenção intention; **ter a intenção de** to have the intention of
intenso/a intense; *(rain)* heavy
interessante interesting
internacional international
intervalo interval; break
intoxicação alimentar food poisoning
inútil useless
Inverno winter
ir to go; **ir a Lisboa** to go to Lisbon; **ir-se embora** to go away; **ir ter com** to meet; **ir com** to go with; **vamos!** let's go!
Irlanda Ireland
irlandês/esa Irish
irmã sister
irmão brother
irritação de pele rash
irritado/a irritated; annoyed
isqueiro lighter
isso that; **isso!** there you go!; **e é por isso que** that is why; **nem por isso** not really
isto this; **isto é** that is to say
IVA VAT

J

já already; now; at once; **já não há ...** there isn't any more ...; **é para já!** coming up!; **já esteve em Portugal?** have you ever been to Portugal?
Janeiro January
janela window
jantar *(n)* dinner
jantar *(v)* to have dinner
jardim garden
jardim botânico botanical garden
jardim zoológico zoo
jarra jug
joalharia jeweller's
joelho knee
jogar to play
jogo match; game
jóias jewellery
jornal newspaper
jovem young

Julho July
Junho June
juntos/as together
justo/a just

lá there; **lá está ela** there she is; **sei lá** I have no idea
lã wool
lábio lip
lado side; **ao lado de** beside
ladrão/ladra thief
lago lake
lama mud
lamentar to regret
lâmina de barbear razor blade
lâmpada light bulb
lanche snack
lanterna torch
lápis pencil
laranja orange
lareira fireplace
largo/a large; wide
lata can, tin
lavandaria launderette
lavandaria a seco dry cleaner's
lavar to wash; **lavar a cabeça** to wash one's hair; **lavar a roupa** to do the washing; **lavar a louça** to do the washing-up; **lavar-se** to have a wash
lavatório lavatory
legendado/a subtitled
legume vegetable
leite milk
lembrança souvenir
lembrar to remind
lembrar-se (de) to remember
lenço (da mão) handkerchief
lenço de papel tissue
lençol sheet
lenha firewood
lente lens
lentes de contacto contact lenses; **lentes de contacto moles/rígidas** soft/hard contact lenses

lento/a slow
ler to read
leste east; **a leste de** (to the) east of; **no leste** in the east
letra letter; handwriting
levantar (money) to withdraw
levantar-se to get up; **levantar voo** to take off
levar to carry; to take; **leva duas horas** it takes two hours; **para levar** to take away
leve light
lhe(s) you; it; her; him; them; **perguntei-lhe** I asked him/her/you; **perguntei-lhes** I asked them/you; **bati-lhe** I hit it (see *grammar*)
ligação connection
ligado/a on (*TV, light*)
ligadura bandage
ligar to plug in; to switch on; (*phone*) to call
limpar to clean
limpeza cleaning
limpo/a clean
lindo/a beautiful
língua tongue; language
linha line; thread; platform
linha do metro underground line
líquido/a liquid
lista list
lista telefónica phone book
litro litre
livraria bookshop
livre free
livro book; **livro de cheques** chequebook
lixo waste; rubbish
logo: até logo see you later; **logo à noite** this evening; **logo que** as soon as; **mais logo** later
loja shop
longe far; **longe de** far from; **muito longe** far away
longo/a long
louça dishes
lua moon
lua-de-mel honeymoon

lugar place; seat; **há lugar para a minha mala?** is there room for my suitcase?
lume fire; light; **tem lume?** do you have a light?; **ao lume** by the fire
luva glove
luxo luxury; **de luxo** luxury
luz light

M

madeira wood
mãe mother
magro/a thin; slim; *(milk)* skimmed
Maio May
mais more; **mais de** more than; **muito mais** much more, a lot more; **mais alguma coisa?** would you like anything else?
mal bad; badly; hardly; **dormi mal** I slept badly; **mal se vê** you can hardly see it; **nada mal** not bad
mala suitcase; **fazer as malas** to pack
mala do carro (car) boot
mal-educado/a rude
mal-entendido misunderstanding
mama breast
mancha stain
mandar to order; to send; **mandar vir** *(in restaurant)* to order; **mandar pelo correio** to post
maneira way; **de qualquer maneira** anyway
manga sleeve
manhã morning
manter to keep; **manter-se** to remain
mão hand
mapa map
máquina machine
máquina de barbear electric shaver
máquina de lavar louça dishwasher
máquina de lavar roupa washing machine
máquina digital digital camera
máquina fotográfica camera
mar sea

marcha-atrás reverse gear
Março March
marco do correio postbox
maré-alta high tide
maré-baixa low tide
marido husband
marina marina
marisco seafood
mas but
matar to kill
material material
matrícula do carro registration number
mau/má bad; **mau tempo** bad weather
máximo/a maximum
me me; *(reflexive)* myself; **não me digas** don't tell me; **ele conhece-me** he knows me; **magoei-me** I hurt myself (see *grammar*)
medicamento medicine
médico/a doctor
médio/a medium; **a média** the average
medo fear; **ter medo de** to be afraid of
meias socks
meia-hora half an hour
meia-noite midnight
meia-pensão half board
meia-volta U-turn; **dar meia-volta** to turn back
meio/a half; middle; **no meio (de)** in the middle (of); **meio litro/quilo** half a litre/kilo
meio-dia midday
mel honey
melhor best; better; **o/a melhor** the best; **é melhor ...** it's better to ...
melhorar to get better
membro member
menos less; least; **o/a menos** the least; **pelo menos** at least; **menos de** less than
mensagem message
menstruação period(s)
mentir to lie
mercado market
mercearia grocer's
mergulhar to dive

mergulho diving; **fazer mergulho** to do scuba diving
mês month
mesa table
mesmo/a the same; **dá no mesmo** it is the same; **faço-o eu mesmo** I'll do it myself; **mesmo se** even if
mesquita mosque
metade half
metro metre; *(transport)* underground
meu(s)/minha(s) my; mine; **um amigo meu** a friend of mine; **os meus/as minhas estão aqui** mine are here; **esse é o meu lugar** that's my seat (see *grammar*)
microondas microwave
mim me; **é para mim** it's for me (see *grammar*)
minha(s) see **meu(s)**
mínimo/a minimum
minuto minute
miradouro viewpoint
missa mass
mochila backpack, rucksack
moda fashion
modo way; **de qualquer modo** in any case
moderno/a modern
moeda coin; currency
moinho mill
molhado/a wet
momento moment; **no momento** at the moment
montanha mountain
monte hill
monumento monument
morada address
mordedura bite
morder to bite
morno/a lukewarm
morrer to die
morto/a dead
mosca fly
mosquito mosquito
mosteiro monastery
mostrar to show

moto motorbike
motor engine
motorista driver
motorizada motorbike
mourisco/a Moorish
mouro/a Moor
mover to move; **mover-se** to move (oneself)
muçulmano/a muslim
mudança change
mudar to change; *(room, place)* to move; **mudar de roupa** to change (clothes)
mudo/a mute
muito(s)/muita(s) very; many; **muito contente** very happy; **muitas vezes** many times, often; **muito(s)/a(s) (de)** a lot (of)
mulher woman
multa fine
mundo world
muralha wall; rampart
muro (external) wall
músculo muscle
museu museum
música music

N

nacionalidade nationality
nada nothing; **de nada** not at all, you're welcome
nadar to swim
namorado/a boyfriend/girlfriend
não no; not; **não, obrigado/a** no, thank you; **não faço ideia** no idea; **ainda não** not yet; **não faz mal** it doesn't matter; **eu também não** neither do I
não fumador(a) non-smoker
nariz nose
nascer to be born; **nasci a .../em ...** I was born on …/in …
nascer-do-sol sunrise
natação swimming
Natal Christmas; **Feliz Natal!** Happy Christmas!
natureza nature

necessário/a necessary

negativo negative *(of photo)*

negócios business

negro/a black

nem neither; nor; **nem … nem …** neither … nor …; **nem eu** neither do I

nenhum(a) none; **não faço ideia nenhuma** I have absolutely no idea

nevar to snow

neve snow

nevoeiro fog

ninguém nobody

nódoa stain

nódoa negra bruise

noite night; evening; **à noite** in the evening; **durante a noite** at nightime, during the night; **boa noite!** good night!

noiva fiancée

noivo fiancé

nome name

nome completo full name

nome de baptismo first name

nome de família family name

normal normal

norte north; **a norte de** (to the) north of; **no norte** in the north

nos us; *(reflexive)* ourselves; **ele conhece -nos** he knows us; **magoámo-nos** we hurt ourselves *(see grammar)*

nós we

nosso(s)/a(s) ours; **um amigo nosso** a friend of ours; **são nossos/as** they are ours; **os nossos/as nossas estão aqui** ours are here *(see grammar)*

nota note; banknote

notícias news

Novembro November

novo/a new; young; **de novo** again

nu(a) naked

número number

número de telefone phone number

nunca never; **nunca mais** never again

nuvem cloud

O

o(s) *(art)* the *(see grammar)*

o(s) *(pron)* it; him; you; them; **eu conheço-o(s)** I know him/you/them; **deixei-o no quarto** I left it in the room *(see grammar)*

obras works; **em obras** under construction

obrigado/a thanks; **muito obrigado/a** thank you very much

obturação *(in tooth)* filling

ocasião occasion

oceano ocean

oculista optician

óculos glasses

óculos de sol sunglasses

óculos (protectores) goggles

ocupado/a busy

ocupar to occupy; to take up; **ocupa muito espaço** it takes up a lot of space; **ocupar-se de** to deal with

oeste west; **a oeste de** (to the) west of; **no oeste** in the west

oferecer to offer

oficina garage

ok OK

olá hello, hi

óleo oil

olhar to look; **olhar para** to look at; to stare at

olho eye

ombro shoulder

onda wave

onde where; **onde é/são …?** where is/are …?; **de onde é?** where are you from?; **para onde vão?** where are you going?

ontem yesterday; **ontem à noite** yesterday evening

ópera opera

operar to operate

opinião opinion; **na minha opinião** in my opinion

oportunidade opportunity

óptimo/a great
orelha ear
orgânico/a organic
organizar to organize; to arrange
origem origin
orquestra orchestra
osso bone
ou or
ouro gold; **de/em ouro** (made of) gold
Outono autumn
outro(s)/outra(s) other; another; **outra vez** again; **os outros/as outras** the others
Outubro October
ouvido ear
ouvir to hear; to listen
ovo egg

P

pacote packet
padaria bakery
padeiro baker
padre priest
pagar to pay
pai father
pais parents
país country
paisagem landscape; scenery
País de Gales Wales
palácio palace
palavra word
palavrão swear word
pálido/a pale
panela pot
pano cloth; fabric
pano da louça tea towel
pão bread
papel paper
papel-higiénico toilet paper
papelaria stationer's
par pair; **um par de sapatos** a pair of shoes
para for; **andar para a frente** to move forward
parabéns congratulations; **dar os**

parabéns a alguém to congratulate someone
pára-brisas windscreen
pára-choques bumper
paragem de autocarro bus stop
paragem de eléctrico tram stop
parar to stop; **sem parar** without stopping
parecer to seem; **parece que ...** it seems that ...; **parecer-se com** to look like; **o que te parece?** what do you think?
parque park
parque de atracções theme park
parque de campismo campsite
parque de estacionamento car park
parte part; **fazer parte de** to be a part of
partida (n) departure; game; **partida de futebol** football match
partido/a (adj) broken
partilhar to share
partir to leave; to break; **partir a perna** to break one's leg; **a partir de segunda-feira** from Monday onwards
parvo/a stupid
Páscoa Easter; **Boa Páscoa!** Happy Easter!
passado (n) past
passado/a (adj) last; **o ano passado** last year
passageiro/a passenger
passagem way (through); **estar de passagem** to be passing through
passagem de nível level crossing
passagem para peões pedestrian crossing
passagem subterrânea subway; underpass
passaporte passport
passar to pass
passar a ferro to iron
pássaro bird
passe pass; season ticket
passear to stroll; **ir passear** to go for a stroll/a walk

passeio promenade; walk
pasta folder; briefcase
pasta de dentes toothpaste
pastilha elástica chewing gum
patins em linha rollerblades
pato duck
paz peace; **deixe-me em paz!** leave me alone!
pé foot; **a pé** by foot; **(mesmo) ao pé de** (just) next to
peão pedestrian
peça piece; part
peça de teatro play
peça sobresselente spare part
pedaço bit; piece
pediatra paediatrician
pedido request; *(in restaurant)* order
pedir to ask; *(in restaurant)* to order; **pedir um favor** to ask a favour; **pedir emprestado/a** to borrow
pedra stone
peito chest
peixaria fishmonger's
peixe fish
pele skin
pêlo hair
pena pity; *(of bird)* feather; **é uma pena** it's a pity; **vale a pena** it's worth it
pensão guest house
pensão completa full board
pensar to think; **pensar (em)** to think about
penso dressing
penso higiénico sanitary towel
pente comb
pequeno/a small; little
pequeno-almoço breakfast; **tomar o pequeno-almoço** to have breakfast
pêra pear
percurso route
perdão forgiveness; **perdão?** pardon?
perder to lose; *(flight, train)* to miss; **perder-se** to get lost; **perder tempo** to waste time
perdido/a lost
perfume perfume

pergunta question
perguntar to ask; **fazer uma pergunta** to ask a question
perigoso/a dangerous
período period; **estar com o período** to have one's period
perna leg
perto near, close by; **perto da praia** near the beach; **o/a ... mais perto** the nearest ...
peru turkey
pesado/a heavy
pescar to fish
pescoço neck
pessoa person
pia washbasin
piada joke
picada *(n)* bite; sting
picado/a *(adj)* stung; bitten; **ser picado/a (por)** to get stung (by); to be bitten (by)
picar to bite; to sting
pijama pyjamas
pilha battery; pile
pílula pill; **tomar a pílula** to be on the pill
pílula do dia seguinte morning-after pill
pinça tweezers
pior worse; **é pior (que)** it's worse (than); **o/a pior** the worst
piorar to get worse
piquenique picnic; **fazer um piquenique** to have a picnic
piscina swimming pool
pista track
placa plate; *(on road)* sign
placa eléctrica hotplate
plano *(n)* plan
plano/a *(adj)* flat
planta plant
plástico plastic
pneu tyre
pneu sobresselente spare tyre
pó powder
pobre poor
poder to be able to; **não posso** I can't
pois because; **pois é!** exactly!

polícia police; *(person)* policeman/policewoman
poluição pollution
pomada ointment
ponte bridge
ponto point; dot; **duas horas em ponto** two o'clock on the dot
por by; per; for; **feito por** made by; **por cento** percent; **por hora** per hour; **por dois dias** for two days
pôr to put
pôr-do-sol sunset
por que...? why...?
porque because
porquê...? why...?
porreiro great
porta door
porta-bagagem boot
porta de embarque gate
portagem toll
portão gate
portátil portable
porto port; harbour
português/esa Portuguese
possível possible
postal postcard
póster poster
posto de gasolina petrol station
posto de turismo tourist office
pouco(s)/a(s) little; few; **pouco tempo** little time; **uns poucos** a few; **um pouco (de)** a bit (of)
poupar to save
pousada da juventude youth hostel
povo people
praça square
praia beach
prancha de surf surfboard
prata silver
prateado/a silver-plated
praticar to practise
prato plate; dish; **prato do dia** dish of the day
prazer pleasure; **muito prazer!** nice to meet you!
precisar (de) to need

preço price
preencher to fill in, to fill out
preferir to prefer
prémio prize
prenda gift, present
preocupação worry
preocupar(-se) to worry; **não se preocupe** don't worry
preparar to prepare
presente present
preservativo condom
preso/a stuck
pressa hurry; **estar com pressa** to be in a hurry
pressão pressure
prestes: estar prestes a to be about to
preto/a black
prevenir to prevent; to warn
previsão do tempo weather forecast
Primavera spring
primeiro/a first; **primeiro ...** first (of all) ...
primeira classe first class
primo/a cousin
principal main
principiante beginner
privado/a private
problema problem
procissão procession
procurar to look for; **procurar fazer** to try to do
produto product
professor(a) teacher
profissão profession
profundo/a deep
programa programme
progresso progress; **fazer progressos** to make progress
proibido/a forbidden
prometer to promise
promoção promotion
pronto/a ready; **estar pronto** to be ready
pronúncia accent
pronunciar to pronounce
propor to propose
propósito: de propósito on purpose

proprietário/a owner

próprio/a own; **o meu próprio carro** my own car; **eu/tu próprio** myself/ yourself

protector solar sun cream

proteger to protect; **proteger-se** to protect oneself

protestante protestant

provar *(fact)* to prove; *(food)* to try, to taste; *(clothes)* to try on

próximo/a next; close; **sou o próximo** I'm next; **próximo da janela** close to the window

publicidade publicity; advertising

público/a public

pulmão lung

pulseira bracelet

pulso wrist; pulse; **medir o pulso** to take one's pulse

puxar to pull

Q

quadrado/a square

quadro painting

qual/quais which; **o/a qual** which; **qual/quais?** which one/ones?

qualidade quality; **de boa/má qualidade** of good/poor quality

qualquer any; **qualquer coisa** anything; **qualquer um/pessoa** anyone

quando when

quanto how much; **quanto custa?** how much is it?; **o quanto antes** as soon as possible; **há quanto tempo?** *(for)* how long?

quarta-feira Wednesday

quarto room; quarter; **quarto das visitas** guest room; **um quarto de hora** a quarter of an hour

quase almost

que that; what; **o que é?** what is it?; **penso que** I think that

quê: não tem de quê not at all; don't mention it

queimadura burn

queimadura solar sunburn

queimar to burn; **queimar-se** to burn oneself

queixar-se to complain

queixo chin

quem who; **quem fala?** who's calling?

quente warm; hot; **uma bebida quente** a hot drink

querer to want; **querer fazer alguma coisa** to want to do something; **querer dizer** to mean; **eu queria …** I would like …; **sem querer** unintentionally

querido/a dear

quilo kilo

quilómetro kilometre

quinta-feira Thursday

quiosque (de jornais) newsagent

R

racista racist

radiador radiator

rádio radio

radiografia X-ray

rainha queen

raio ray

rapar to shave

rapariga girl

rapaz boy

rápido/a fast, quick

raquete racket

raro/a rare; **raras vezes** seldom

ratazana rat

rato mouse

razoável reasonable

realidade reality

rebentar to burst

rebocar to tow

reboque breakdown truck

recarregar to recharge

receber to receive

receita recipe; *(medical)* prescription

recente recent

recepção reception

recepcionista receptionist

recibo receipt

reclamar to complain
recomendar to recommend
reconhecer to recognize
recordação souvenir
recordar-se to remember
recusar to refuse
redondo/a round
redução reduction
reduzir to reduce
reembolsar to refund; **ser reembolsado/a** to get a refund
reembolso refund
refeição meal
refúgio refuge
região region
regressar to come back; to return
regresso return
rei king
Reino Unido United Kingdom
religião religion
relógio clock
relógio de pulso watch
relva grass
remetente sender
reparação repair
reparar to repair; **mandar reparar alguma coisa** to get something repaired; **reparar em** to notice
repetir to repeat
rés-do-chão ground floor
reservado/a reserved
reservar to book, to reserve
respirador snorkel
responder to answer
resposta answer
ressaca hangover
restaurante restaurant
retrato portrait
reumatismo rheumatism
reunião meeting
revelar to reveal; **mandar revelar** (photos) to develop
revista magazine
ria estuary
rico/a rich
rim kidney

rio river
rir to laugh
risco risk; line
rocha rock
rochedo cliff
roda wheel; **andar à roda** to turn
roda sobresselente spare wheel
rodoviária bus station
rolo film
romance novel; romance
ropão bathrobe
rosa rose
rosto face
rotunda roundabout
roubar to steal
roubo theft; rip-off
roupa clothes
roupa interior underwear
rua street
ruínas ruins
ruivo/a a red

S

sábado Saturday
sabão soap
saber to know; to taste; **não sei nadar** I can't swim; **não sei** I don't know; **saber a** to taste like; **saber bem/mal** to taste good/bad
sabonete soap
sabor flavour; taste
saca de plástico plastic bag
saca-rolhas corkscrew
saco bag
saco do lixo rubbish bag
saco-cama sleeping bag
saia skirt
saída exit; way out
saída de emergência emergency exit
sair to come out; to go out; **sair com alguém** to go out with someone
sal salt
sala de concertos concert hall
sala de estar living room
saldos sales

salgado/a salty
salto jump; (of shoe) heel; **usar saltos altos** to wear high heels
salvar to save
sandálias sandals
sangrar to bleed
sangue blood
sanitários toilets
santinho/a! bless you!
santo/a saint
sapatilhas trainers
sapatos shoes
satisfeito/a pleased
saudade: sentir/ter saudades de to miss
saúde health; **saúde!** cheers!
se (pron) itself; himself; herself; yourself; oneself; yourselves; themselves; **magoou-se?** did you hurt yourself?; **elas magoaram-se** they hurt themselves (see grammar)
se (adv) if; **se bem que** although; **se faz favor** please; **se não se importa** if you don't mind
sé cathedral
seca drought; (person, thing) bore; **é uma seca** it's a bore
secador de cabelo hairdryer
secar to dry
secção section
seco/a dry
século century
seda silk
sede thirst; **ter sede** to be thirsty
segredo secret
seguir to follow
segunda-feira Monday
segundo/a second
segunda classe second class
segurança safety, security
segurar to hold; **segurar-se** to hold on
seguro (n) insurance
seguro/a (adj) safe; secure; sure
selo stamp
sem without; **sem glúten** gluten-free
semáforos traffic lights

semana week; **durante a semana** during the week; **toda a semana** all week
sempre always; **sempre em frente** straight ahead, straight on; **sempre que** every time (that)
senão otherwise
senhor Mr; sir; **o(s) senhor(es)** you
senhora Mrs; madam; **a(s) senhora(s)** you
sensato sensible
sensível sensitive
sentar-se to sit down
sentido sense; direction
sentimento feeling
sentir to feel; **sentir-se bem/mal** to feel good/bad; **sentir-se mal** to feel sick; **sentir falta de** to miss
separado/a separate; separated
separar to separate; **separar-se** to split up
ser to be; **sou professora** I'm a teacher; **ser operado** to have an operation; **a não ser que** unless; **ou seja** I mean; **será que ...** I wonder if ...; **ser capaz de** to be able to; **é possível que chova** it might rain
sério/a serious
sertã frying pan
serviço service
servir to serve; **servir para...** to be good for...; **servir-se de** to help oneself with
seta arrow
Setembro September
seu(s)/sua(s) its; his; hers; your; yours; their; theirs (see grammar)
sexo sex; gender
sexta-feira Friday
si it; itself; her; herself; him; himself; you; yourself; them; themselves (see grammar)
sida AIDS
significar mean; **o que significa ...?** what does ... mean?
silêncio silence
silencioso/a silent
sim yes

simpático/a nice
simples simple
sinagoga synagogue
sinal sign; signal
sinal de trânsito road sign
sítio da Web website
situação situation
só only; alone; **só um** only one; **ele está só** he is alone
sobre about; over; **um livro sobre …** a book about …
sobremesa dessert
sobrenome surname
sociedade society
socorro help; **pedir socorro** to ask for help
sofrer to suffer; **sofrer um acidente** to have an accident
sol sun; **ao sol** in the sun
solo ground; **no solo** on the ground
solteiro/a single
som sound
sombra shade; **à sombra** in the shade
soneca nap; **dormir uma soneca** to have a nap
sonhar to dream
sonho dream
sono sleep; **ter sono** to be sleepy
sorrir to smile
sorriso smile
sorte luck; **boa sorte!** good luck!
sotaque accent
soutiã bra
Sr. Mr
Sra. Mrs; Miss; Ms
sua(s) see **seu(s)**
suar to sweat
suficiente enough
sugerir to suggest
sujar-se to get dirty
sujo/a dirty
sul south; **a sul de** (to the) south of; **no sul** in the south
sumo juice
suor sweat
supermercado supermarket

suplemento supplement
suportar to stand; **não o suporto** I can't stand him
surdo/a deaf
surf surfing; **fazer surf** to go surfing
surpresa surprise

T

tabacaria tobacconist's
tabaco tobacco
taberna pub
tabuleiro tray
taça bowl; cup; **uma taça de champagne** a glass of champagne
tacho saucepan
tal/tais such; **que tal?** what do you think?; how about it?; **tais como …** such as …
talão receipt; ticket
talher cutlery
talho butcher's
talvez maybe, perhaps
tamanho size
também also; **eu também não** me neither
tampa lid; *(of bottle)* top; *(of bathtub, sink)* plug
tampão tampon
tampões para os ouvidos earplugs
tanto(s)/a(s) so many; so much; **tanto melhor** all the better
tão so; **tão caro** so expensive
tapar to cover
tapete rug; mat; carpet
tarde *(n)* afternoon; **boa tarde!** good afternoon!
tarde *(adv)* late; **já é tarde** it's late; **chegar tarde** to arrive late
tarifa normal full fare, full price
tarifa reduzida discount fare
tasca pub
taxa tax
taxa de câmbio exchange rate
táxi taxi
taxista taxi driver

te you; yourself (see *grammar*)

teatro theatre

tecido fabric

teclado keyboard

teleférico ski lift

telefonar to phone, to telephone

telefone phone, telephone

telefonema phone call; **fazer um telefonema** to make a phone call

telefonista switchboard operator

telemóvel mobile (phone)

televisão television

televisão por cabo cable TV

temperatura temperature; **medir a temperatura de alguém** to take someone's temperature

tempestade storm

templo temple

tempo weather; time; **o tempo está mau** the weather's bad; **não tenho tempo** I don't have time

temporário/a temporary

tenda tent

ténis (*sport*) tennis; (*shoes*) trainers

tensão alta high blood pressure

tensão arterial blood pressure

tensão baixa low blood pressure

tentar to try; **tentar fazer alguma coisa** to try to do something

ter to have; **ter dor de cabeça** to have a headache; **tenho de ir** I have to go

terça-feira Tuesday

termas spa

termo Thermos® flask

termómetro thermometer

terra earth; soil

terraço terrace

terramoto earthquake

terrível terrible

tesoura scissors

testa forehead

teu(s)/tua(s) your; yours; **o teu bilhete está aqui** your ticket is here; **as tuas estão aqui** yours are here (see *grammar*)

tigela bowl

ti you; yourself; **escrito por ti** written by you; **é para ti** it's for you (see *grammar*)

tia aunt

tímido/a shy

tio uncle

típico/a typical

tipo kind; type; **que tipo de …?** what kind of …?

tirar to take off; to take from; to take out; to steal

toalha towel

toalha de banho bath towel

toalha de praia beach towel

toalha de rosto hand towel

tocar to touch; (*instrument*) to play; **tocar à campainha** to ring the bell

todo/a whole; all; **o bolo todo** the whole cake; **todo o dia** all day; **toda a gente** everybody; **ao todo** in total

todos/as every; everybody; **todos os dias** every day; **todas as semanas** every week; **todos foram** everybody went

tomada plug

tomar to take; **toma!** take it!; **tomar banhos de sol** to sunbathe

tonturas: sentir/ter tonturas to feel dizzy

topo top; **no topo** at the top

torcer to twist; **torcer o pé** to sprain one's ankle

tornar-se to become

torneira tap

tornozelo ankle

torre tower

tosse cough; **ter tosse** to have a cough

tossir to cough

tourada bullfight

trabalhar to work

trabalho work

tradicional traditional

traduzir to translate

tranquilo/a peaceful

transbordo: fazer transbordo to change

transferência transfer

transferir to transfer
trânsito traffic
transpirar to sweat
transporte público public transport
trás: de trás back; **a porta de trás** the back door
travão brake
travão de mão handbrake
travar to brake
trazer to bring
trilho path; track; **trilho para bicicletas** cycle path
triste sad
trocar to change, to exchange
troco change
trovoada thunderstorm
tu you
tua(s) see **teu(s)**
tubo pipe; tube
tudo all; **tudo incluído** all inclusive
turismo tourism
turista *(n)* tourist
turístico/a *(adj)* tourist

U

último/a last
ultrapassar to overtake
um(a) a; one; **uma vez** once; **uma vez por dia/por hora** once a day/an hour *(see grammar)*
unha nail
União Europeia European Union
urgência emergency; **em caso de urgência** in case of emergency; **urgências** casualty (department)
urgente urgent
usado/a used
usar to use; *(glasses, perfume)* to wear
utente user
útil useful
utilizar to use
uva grape

V

vaca cow
vacinado/a (contra) vaccinated (against)
vagão carriage
vagão-cama sleeping car
vale valley; *(money)* voucher
valer to be worth; **vale a pena** it's worth it
validade validity
válido/a valid
válvula stopcock
varanda balcony
vários/as several
vazio/a empty
vegetariano/a vegetarian
vela candle; *(car)* spark plug; *(sport)* sailing; **fazer vela** to go sailing
velho/a old
velocidade speed; **a toda a velocidade** at full speed
vencedor(a) winner
vendedor(a) shop assistant
vender to sell
vende-se for sale
venenoso/a poisonous
ventilador fan
vento wind
ventoinha fan
ver to see
Verão summer
verdadeiro/a true
verde green; unripe
verga wicker
vergonha shame; embarassment
verificar to check
vermelho/a red
vertigem: ter vertigens to have vertigo
vespa wasp
Vespa® scooter
véspera: na véspera the day before
vestiário cloakroom
vestido dress
vestir to wear; **vestir-se** to get dressed
vez turn; time; **é a sua vez** it's your turn;

às vezes sometimes; **desta vez** this time; **três vezes ao dia** three times a day

via road

via rápida dual carriageway

viagem journey, trip; **boa viagem!** have a good trip!; **viagem de negócios** business trip

viajante traveller; passenger

viajar to travel

viatura vehicle

vida life

vide, videira vine

vídeo video

vidrado/a glazed

vidro glass

vigiar to watch (over)

vila small town

vindima vintage, wine harvest

violação rape; violation

vir to come; **venho de Porto** I come from Porto; **a semana que vem** next week

virar to turn; **virar à esquerda** to turn left

visita visit; tour; visitor

visita guiada guided tour

visitar to visit

vista view; eyesight; **até à vista!** see you!; **ter boa vista** to have a good eyesight; **com vista para o mar** with a sea view

visto visa; **visto de entrada/saída** entry/exit visa

vítima victim; casualty

vitrais stained-glass windows

viúva widow

viúvo widower

vitrine (shop) window

vivenda cottage, villa

viver to live

vivo/a alive

vizinho/a neighbour

voar to fly

você(s) you; yourself; yourselves (see *grammar*)

volante steering wheel

voleibol volleyball

volta turn; return; **estar de volta** to be back; **dar uma volta** to go for a walk; **à volta de** around; **durante a/na volta** on the way back

voltagem voltage

voltar to return; to turn

vomitar to vomit

vontade wish; **contra a vontade** against one's will; **de boa/má vontade** willingly/ reluctantly; **ter vontade de** to want to do something

voo flight

vos you; **apetece-vos dar um passeio?** would you like to go for a walk?

vós you; yourself; yourselves; **feito por vós** done by you (see *grammar*)

vosso(s)/a(s) your; yours; **o vosso bilhete está aqui** your ticket is here; **estes são vossos** these are yours (see *grammar*)

votos wishes; **votos de boas festas** seasons greetings; **votos de felicidades** best wishes

voz voice; **em voz alta/baixa** loudly/ quietly

WXZ

WC das senhoras ladies' (toilet)

WC dos homens gents' (toilet)

windsurf windsurfing; **fazer windsurf** to go windsurfing

xadrez chess

xale, xaile shawl

xarope syrup

zangado/a angry

zero zero

zona area

zona pedonal pedestrianized area

GRAMMAR

The definite and indefinite articles in Portuguese change according to gender and number, ie singular or plural noun:

	definite article (the)		indefinite article (a/an)	
	singular	plural	singular	plural
masculine	**o**	**os**	**um**	**uns**
feminine	**a**	**as**	**uma**	**umas**

The contractions with the definite article and the prepositions **a**, **de**, **em** and **por** are as follows:

a + o = ao	**a + os = aos**
a + a = à	**a + as = às**
de + o = do	**de + os = dos**
de + a = da	**de + as = das**
em + o = no	**em + os = nos**
em + a = na	**em + as = nas**
por + o = pelo	**por + os = pelos**
por + a = pela	**por + as = pelas**

The indefinite article can be contracted with the prepositions **em** and **de**, but this contraction is not compulsory.

em + um = num	**de + um = dum**
em + uma = numa	**de + uma = duma**

There are two genders in Portuguese. The majority of **nouns** ending in **o** are masculine, whereas most of those ending in **a** are feminine. The majority of nouns ending in **ã**, **em** and **ade** are feminine, as well as those ending in **ão**, though a fair number of these are masculine:

eg	feminine	masculine
	canção song	**irmão** brother
	estação station	**pão** bread
	pensão guesthouse	**cão** dog

A number of words ending in **a** and **e** are both masculine and feminine: **o/a gerente** the manager, **o/a doente** the patient, **o/a polícia** the policeman/policewoman, **o/a guia** the guide.

As a general rule, the plural of the noun is formed by adding an **s** at the end. The plural of nouns ending with **r**, **s** or **z** is created by adding **es** to the end. The plural of the nouns that end in **ão**, according to each case, may be formed in three different ways: mão → **mãos**, cão → **cães**, coração → **corações**.

The plural of nouns which end in **m** is formed as follows: nuvem → **nuvens**, boletim → **boletins**, som →**sons**, jejum → **jejuns** and the plural of nouns which end in **l** as follows: hotel → **hotéis**, anel → **anéis**. As for the nouns which end in **ês**, the plural is **eses**: inglês→ **ingleses**.

Adjectives agree with the gender and number of the noun which they describe. They are usually placed after the noun:

a flor amarela	the yellow flower
os limões amarelos	the yellow lemons

Adjectives which end in **o** are made feminine by replacing the **o** with an **a**. In general, adjectives which end in **ão** are made feminine by replacing **ão** with **ã**. An **a** is added to the end of adjectives which end in **u** and **or**:

cru → crua   acolhedor → acolhedora

Adjectives which end in **ês** are made feminine by replacing the **ês** with **esa**: português → portuguesa.

The plural of adjectives is formed in the same way as nouns.

Comparatives are used according to the formula **mais/menos ... do que ... tão ... como ...**:

o hotel Sol é mais confortável do que o hotel Lua
the hotel Sol is more comfortable than the hotel Lua

a comida é tão boa como a deste hotel
the food is as good as the food at this hotel

As a rule, superlatives are formed by adding a definite article to the formula **mais/menos**:

o mais caro dos dois é o hotel Lua
the most expensive of the two is the hotel Lua

quais são os mais baratos?
which are the cheapest?

The following are some common adjectives with irregular comparatives and superlatives:

bom/boa good	**melhor** better	**o/a melhor** the best
grande big	**maior** bigger	**o/a maior** the biggest
mau/má bad	**pior** worse	**o/a pior** the worst

As the name suggests, **demonstratives** indicate people, objects or animals: **este**, **esta**, **estes** and **estas** are used when the person or object is near to the speaker. By contrast, **esse**, **essa**, **esses**, **essas** are used when the person or object is near to the listener and **essas**, **aquele**, **aquela**, **aqueles** and **aquelas** are used when the person or object is further away from both the speaker and the listener. There are three unchanging demonstratives: **isto**, **isso** and **aquilo**:

isto é uma maçã	this is an apple
isso é para amanhã	that is for tomorrow
o que é aquilo além?	what is that over there?

Possessive pronouns

	masculine	feminine
mine	o meu	a minha
yours	o teu	a tua
his/hers/its	o seu/dele*	a sua/dela*
ours	o nosso	a nossa
yours	o vosso	a vossa
theirs	o seu/deles*	a sua/delas*

Possessive adjectives

	masculine	feminine
my	meu	minha
your	teu	tua
his/her/its	seu/dele*	seu/dela*
our	nosso	nossa
your	vosso	vossa
their	seu/deles*	sua/delas*

*****dele** and **dela** are mostly used in spoken Portuguese. For example, instead of **a sua casa**, it is more usual to say **a casa dele**.

> este é o meu lugar e o seu é aquele
> this is my seat and yours is that one

> esse é o teu livro e o deles é este
> that is your book and theirs is this one

> o vosso quarto é maior do que o nosso
> your room is bigger than ours

In order to form the plural, you just need to add an **s**:

> estes são os teus livros e esses são os meus
> these are your books and those are mine

Personal pronouns

subject		added to verb*		after preposition	
eu	I	**me**	me	**mim**	me
tu	you *(informal)*	**te**	you *(informal)*	**ti**	you *(informal)*
você	you *(formal)*	**o/a/lhe**	you *(formal)*	**si/você**	you *(formal)*
ele	he/it	**o/lhe**	him/it	**ele**	him/it
ela	she/it	**a/lhe**	her/it	**ela**	her/it
nós	we	**nos**	us	**nós**	us
vós	you *(formal)*	**os/as/lhes**	you *(formal)*	**vós**	you *(formal)*
vocês	you *(informal)*	**vos/lhes**	you *(informal)*	**vocês**	you *(informal)*
eles	they	**os/lhes**	them	**eles**	them
elas	they	**as/lhes**	them	**elas**	them

*In affirmatives these are added to the verb with a hyphen and in negative sentences they are positioned before the verb. In some instances they contract and become **mo**, **ma**, **to**, **ta**, **lo**, **la**, **lho**, **lha**.

desculpem, não **os** vi	sorry, I didn't see you
ela mostrou-**lhes** as fotografias	she showed them the photos
ele deu o livro a **mim**	he gave the book to me
ele deu-**me** o livro	he gave me the book
eles ainda não **lhe** telefonaram?	they haven't phoned you yet?
guardei um para **si**	I saved one for you
os bilhetes, dei-**lhos** ontem	the tickets, I gave them to you yesterday
prazer em conhecê-**la**	pleased to meet you

Tu is used to address friends, close relatives or children. **Você**, **o senhor** and **a senhora** are used in more formal situations and to address people you don't know well. **Tu** conjugates as the second person singular while **você**, **o senhor** and **a senhora** are conjugated as the third person singular.

> eu vou perguntar à Rita se tu podes ir à festa dela
> I'll ask Rita if you can go to her party

> você/o senhor é médico?   os senhores moram em Lisboa?
> are you a doctor?   do you live in Lisbon?

After some prepositions, the personal pronoun contracts:

> em + **ele/ela** = **nele/nela**   com + **si** = **consigo**
> com + **mim** = **comigo**   com + **nós** = **conosco**

com + ti = **contigo**   com + vós = **convosco**

Reflexive pronouns:

me	myself	**nos**	ourselves
te	yourself (*informal*)	**vos**	yourselves
se	himself; herself; itself; oneself; yourself (*formal*); yourselves; themselves		

eu vejo-**me** no espelho I see myself in the mirror
sirva-**se**/sirvam-**se**, se faz favor please, help youself/yourselves
ele/ela não **se** magoou he/she did not hurt himself/herself

Personal subject pronouns can be dropped in Portuguese as the **verb** ending designates the subject, eg almoço às 12.30 I eat at 12.30pm.

Portuguese verbs end in **ar**, **er** or **ir** in the infinitive. Regular verbs will have the following endings in the present simple:

	andar	comer	partir
eu	ando	como	parto
tu	andas	comes	partes
ele/ela	anda	come	parte
nós	andamos	comemos	partimos
vós	andais	comeis	partis
eles/elas	andam	comem	partem

The irregular verbs **ser** and **estar** both mean "to be". **Ser** indicates an inherent or permanent state, quality or characteristic and is used with occupations, nationalities and to tell the time and refer to permanent location. **Estar** indicates a non-permanent state, action or place:

está a chover	it's raining
estou em Londres	I am in London
onde é o aeroporto?	where is the airport?
são nove horas	it's nine o'clock
sou estudante/apenas um turista	I am student/just a tourist
sou português	I am Portuguese

In the same way, there are two verbs which mean "to have" in Portuguese. **Ter** indicates possession, **haver** is mostly used in the third person to mean "there is":

tenho um carro	I have a car
há pouca gente no hotel	there are few people in the hotel
há caracóis	there are snails (on the menu)

As in other languages, irregular verbs in Portuguese can be learned as they appear.

The conjugation of **fazer** to make, **ir** to go, **pedir** to ask, **poder** to be able to and **querer** to want, will certainly be useful:

	eu	tu	ele/ela	nós	vós	eles/elas
ser	sou	és	é	somos	sois	são
estar	estou	estás	está	estamos	estais	estão
ter	tenho	tens	tem	temos	tendes	têm
fazer	faço	fazes	faz	fazemos	fazeis	fazem
ir	vou	vais	vai	vamos	ides	vão
pedir	peço	pedes	pede	pedimos	pedis	pedem
poder	posso	podes	pode	podemos	podeis	podem
querer	quero	queres	quer	queremos	quereis	querem

The past simple and the past continuous are the most commonly used past forms. The first indicates that an action is completely finished, eg "I did something", the latter indicates an action which occurred over a period of time in the past, but no longer does so, eg "I used to do something". Here are the conjugations of the regular verbs:

Past Simple

	andar	comer	partir
eu	andei	comi	parti
tu	andaste	comeste	partiste
ele/ela	andou	comeu	partiu
nós	andámos	comemos	partimos
vós	andastes	comestes	partistes
eles/elas	andaram	comeram	partiram

Past Continuous

	andar	comer	partir
eu	andava	comia	partia
tu	andavas	comias	partias
ele/ela	andava	comia	partia
nós	andávamos	comíamos	partíamos
vós	andáveis	comíeis	partíeis
eles/elas	andavam	comiam	partiam

... and of certain irregular verbs:

Past Simple

	eu	tu	ele/ela	nós	vós	eles/elas
ser	fui	foste	foi	fomos	fostes	foram
estar	estive	estiveste	esteve	estivemos	estivestes	estiveram
ter	tive	tiveste	teve	tivemos	tivestes	tiveram
fazer	fiz	fizeste	fez	fizemos	fizestes	fizeram
ir	fui	foste	foi	fomos	fostes	foram
pedir	pedi	pediste	pediu	pedimos	pedistes	pediram
poder	pude	pudeste	pôde	pudemos	pudestes	puderam
querer	quis	quiseste	quis	quisemos	quisestes	quiseram

Past Continuous

	eu	tu	ele/ela	nós	vós	eles/elas
ser	era	eras	era	éramos	éreis	eram
estar	estava	estavas	estava	estávamos	estáveis	estiveram
ter	tinha	tinhas	tinha	tínhamos	tínheis	tinham
fazer	fazia	fazias	fazia	fazíamos	fazíeis	faziam
ir	ia	ias	ia	íamos	íeis	iam
pedir	pedia	pedias	pedia	pedíamos	pedíeis	pediam
poder	podia	podias	podia	podíamos	podíeis	podiam
querer	queria	querias	queria	queríamos	queríeis	queriam

For the **future simple**, the verbs conjugate in the following manner:

	andar	comer	partir
eu	and**arei**	com**erei**	part**irei**
tu	and**arás**	com**erás**	part**irás**
ele/ela	and**ará**	com**erá**	part**irá**
nós	and**aremos**	com**eremos**	part**iremos**
vós	and**areis**	com**ereis**	part**ireis**
eles/elas	and**arão**	com**erão**	part**irão**

In order to form the **negative** in Portuguese, it is sufficient to place **não** in front of the verb:

não conheço Lisboa	I do not know Lisbon

Intonation is sufficient to turn a statement from an affirmation into a **question**:

o quarto tem duas camas	the room has two beds
o quarto tem duas camas?	does the room have two beds?

HOLIDAYS AND FESTIVALS

BANK HOLIDAYS

Bank holidays are known as **feriados** and working days are called **dias úteis**. On bank holidays, administrative offices, banks and most shops are closed. The following is a list of Portugal's official holidays:

1 January	New Year's Day
February	Carnival
March/April	Good Friday
25 April	Celebration of the 1974 revolution (the "Carnation Revolution")
1 May	Labour Day
May/June	Corpus Christi
10 June	Day of Portugal, Camões and the Communities
15 August	Assumption
5 October	Anniversary of the Republic
1 November	All Saints' Day
1 December	Restoration of Portuguese Independence (1640)
8 December	Immaculate Conception
25 December	Christmas Day

ANNUAL FESTIVALS AND EVENTS

Spring and autumn are the best times to experience local culture. The Portuguese remain faithful to tradition, and religious festivals celebrating patron saints (**romarias**) are very important. The following is a list of just some of the many local festivals and events:

January	Festival of **rapazes** (boys) in Bragança (first week of January)
	Epiphany or **Dia de Reis** celebrated by eating a special crown-shaped cake (**bolo-rei**) containing dried fruit and a hidden lucky charm

February	**Fantasporto**, large science-fiction film festival held in Porto (second week of February)
	Popular carnivals in Ovar and Torres Vedras with processions of floats
March	**OviBeja**, large agricultural fair featuring gastronomy, handicrafts and horse racing in Beja in the Alentejo
March/April	Easter Week/Holy Week: processions and religious ceremonies in Braga (**Senhor Ecce Homo**)
	Easter Sunday: pilgrimage to Nossa Senhora da Piedade and to Loulé in the Algarve
Mid-April	**FIAPE**, international agriculture, livestock and craft fair in Estremoz
	Festival of **cruzes** (crosses) in Barcelos (Minho)
	Flower festival in Madeira
	Worldwide pilgrimage to Fátima with a torchlit procession and international mass
	Queima das Fitas in Coimbra celebrating the end of the university year
	Pilgrimage to **Bom Jesus** in Braga (Pentecost)
May-June	**Festroia**, international film festival held in Setúbal
June	Festival of **São Gonçalo** in Amarante (first weekend of June)
	National agricultural fair in Santarém
	12–19 June: festival of the saints of Lisbon, featuring the Saint Anthony **marchas**
	23 and 24 June: festival of **São João** (St John) in Porto, Braga and Vila do Conde, where a procession of lacemakers takes place
	28 and 29 June: festival of **São Pedro** (St Peter) in Sintra, Évora, Vila Real and Póvoa de Varzim
July	Festival of the **tabuleiros** (trays) in Tomar (first week of July, every 4 years)
	Colete encarnado (red waistcoat) festival in Vila Franca de Xira

	Ria festival with a competition for the best-decorated **moliceiro** boat, held in Aveiro **Vilar de Mouros** Festival, the most famous rock festival in Portugal, usually takes place in the second half of July **Rainha Santa Isabel** Festival, held on even numbered years in Coimbra, often coinciding with the town's holiday on 4 July
August	**Gualterianas** festival in Guimarães (first weekend of August) Festival of the **Senhora da Boa Viagem** in Peniche (first weekend of August) Festival of **Nossa Senhora de Agonia** in Viana do Castelo (third week of August)
September	Wine harvesting festival in Palmela (first week of September) Pilgrimage to **Nossa Senhora dos Remédios** in Lamego (8 September) Pilgrimage to **Nossa Senhora do Nazo** in Miranda do Douro (8 September) Festival of **Nossa Senhora da Nazaré** (from 8 September) Festival of **São Mateus** (St Matthew) in Elvas and Viseu (21 September) New Fairs (**Feiras Novas**) of Ponte de Lima, big market and funfair event, featuring processions and folk music, dating back to the 12th Century (mid-September)
October	4–12 October: local craft fair in Vila Franca de Xira, with bull running and bullfighting Festival of gastronomy, crafts and folklore in Santarém Last pilgrimage to Fátima (12 and 13 October)
November	National horse fair and festival of **São Martinho** (St Martin) in Golegã (first two weeks of November)

USEFUL ADDRESSES

IN THE UK:

Portuguese Trade and Tourism Office/ICEP
Portuguese Embassy, 11 Belgrave Square, London SW1X 8PP
Tel.: 0845 355 1212 (brochure line) / 020 7201 6666
Website: www.visitportugal.com

IN PORTUGAL:

Direcção Geral de Turismo
Avenida Antonio Augusto de Aguiar, 86
1069-021 Lisbon
Tel.: 21 358 6400
Website: www.dgturismo.pt

British Embassy
Rua de São Bernardo, 33
1249-082 Lisbon
Tel.: 21 392 4000
Website: www.britishembassy.gov.uk

> **Directory enquiries:** 118
> **Emergency:** 112
> **Plane departures/arrivals information:** 218 413 700
> **Tourist support line:** 800 29696
> **Weather:** 12 150

British Consulate (Algarve)
Largo Francisco A Maurício, 7 - 1º
8500 - 355 Portimão
Tel.: 28 249 0750 (8 lines)
Out of hours line for emergencies involving British citizens only: 96 272 0556

British Consulate (Madeira)
Apartado 417
EC Zarco (Funchal)
9001 - 956 Funchal
Tel.: 291 212 860 to 867
Out of hours line for emergencies involving British citizens only: 96 272 0557

British Consulate (Azores)
Rua Domingos Rebelo, 43
9500 - 234 Ponta Delgada
S. Miguel – Azores
Tel.: 296 628 175

CONVERSION TABLES

Note that when writing numbers, Portuguese uses a comma where English uses a full stop. For example 0.6 would be written 0,6 in Portuguese, and 1,500 would be written 1.500 or 1 500.

Measurements

Only the metric system is used in Portugal.

Length

1 cm ≈ 0.4 inches
30 cm ≈ 1 foot

Distance

1 metre ≈ 1 yard
1 km ≈ 0.6 miles

To convert kilometres into miles, divide by 8 and then multiply by 5.

kilometres	1	2	5	10	20	100
miles	0.6	1.25	3.1	6.25	12.50	62.5

To convert miles into kilometres, divide by 5 and then multiply by 8.

miles	1	2	5	10	20	100
kilometres	1.6	3.2	8	16	32	160

Weight

25g ≈ 1 oz   1 kg ≈ 2 lb   6 kg ≈ 1 stone

To convert kilos into pounds, divide by 5 and then multiply by 11.
To convert pounds into kilos, multiply by 5 and then divide by 11.

kilos	1	2	10	20	60	80
pounds	2.2	4.4	22	44	132	176

Liquid

1 litre ≈ 2 pints
4.5 litres ≈ 1 gallon

Temperature

To convert temperatures in Fahrenheit into Celsius, subtract 32, multiply by 5 and then divide by 9.

To convert temperatures in Celsius into Fahrenheit, divide by 5, multiply by 9 and then add 32.

Fahrenheit (°F)	32	40	50	59	68	86	100
Celsius (°C)	0	4	10	15	20	30	38

Clothes sizes

Sometimes you will find sizes given using the English-language abbreviations **XS** (Extra Small), **S** (Small), **M** (Medium), **L** (Large) and **XL** (Extra Large).

• Women's clothes

Europe	36	38	40	42	44	etc
UK	8	10	12	14	16	

• Bras (cup sizes are the same)

Europe	70	75	80	85	90	etc
UK	32	34	36	38	40	

• Men's shirts (collar size)

Europe	36	38	41	43	etc
UK	14	15	16	17	

• Men's clothes

Europe	40	42	44	46	48	50 etc
UK	30	32	34	36	38	40

Shoe sizes

• Women's shoes

Europe	37	38	39	40	42	etc
UK	4	5	6	7	8	

• Men's shoes

Europe	40	42	43	44	46	etc
UK	7	8	9	10	11	